I0673539

The Occult Arts

Also from Westphalia Press
westphaliapress.org

The Occult Arts

An Examination of the Claims
Made for the Existence of
Supernormal Powers

---

by J. W. Frings

WESTPHALIA PRESS
An Imprint of Policy Studies Organization

The Occult Arts: An Examination of the Claims
Made for the Existence of Supernormal Powers
All Rights Reserved © 2017 by Policy Studies Organization

Westphalia Press
An imprint of Policy Studies Organization
1527 New Hampshire Ave., NW
Washington, D.C. 20036
info@ipsonet.org

ISBN-13: 978-1-63391-609-8
ISBN-10: 1-63391-609-X

Cover design by Jeffrey Barnes:
jbarnesbook.design

Daniel Gutierrez-Sandoval, Executive Director
PSO and Westphalia Press

Updated material and comments on this edition
can be found at the Westphalia Press website:
www.westphaliapress.org

THE OCCULT ARTS

THE
OCCULT ARTS

AN EXAMINATION OF THE CLAIMS MADE
FOR THE EXISTENCE AND PRACTICE OF
SUPERNORMAL POWERS, AND AN
ATTEMPTED JUSTIFICATION OF SOME
OF THEM BY THE CONCLUSIONS OF THE
RESEARCHES OF MODERN SCIENCE

BY

J. W. FRINGS

LONDON
WILLIAM RIDER AND SON, LIMITED
CATHEDRAL HOUSE, PATERNOSTER ROW, E.C.
1913

First Published in September 1918

TO

MY MOTHER

WHOSE BELIEF HAS NEVER WAVERED

PREFACE

IT is hoped that this little book will itself satisfactorily explain its purpose. But a word here may not be out of place, if it be used merely to shew the position of the writer in relation to the subject. Some years of fairly serious study in the bypaths of science and mysticism have produced the mental attitude which compels him to take the view that underlying all the phenomena of the so-called occult, there is a basic force of manifestation which only requires to be investigated to be divested of its mystery and apparently wonderful character.

There is nothing supernatural. Nature is the sum of content. But to many minds there is much that is supernormal to them. The farther up the side of a mountain one ascends, however, the greater is the prospect which appears in view. The more widely one extends the mental vision by the review

7

of further human knowledge, the more easily does the supernormal become the normal. The isolated and seemingly contradictory experience is then simply fitted into its niche in the great scheme of things. It is seen to be the final note in the chord required to complete the harmony of the universe.

J. W. FRINGS.

London, May 23, 1913.

CONTENTS

THE OCCULT ARTS

CHAPTER I

INTRODUCTORY

IT would be difficult to define just exactly what constitutes an occult art. From the ordinary standpoint the term " occult " means secret or hidden. An occult art would therefore be one the principles of which are mysterious and its practice secret. An occult art, then, is one that is not in common use. It will be evident, therefore, that the general intellectual development of a people modifies the term. In savagery the healing art and the art of writing may well be considered occult arts. In a more advanced community the arts of photography, of phonography, (record-making by the Edison or similar machine), of telephony or telegraphy, might all be conceived to be occult arts. In a later stage of civilisation wireless telegraphy, mesmerism, or even aviation might be considered occult arts. It may be inferred, then, that an art widely practised and generally understood has ceased to be an occult art. Conversely an art, or an alleged art, the principles of which are mysterious, or one not generally understood, and which is not ordinarily practised, is an occult art.

There are many alleged arts which fall within the scope of this description—alchemy, astrology, cheiromancy, cheiroscopy, clairvoyance, clairaudience, geomancy, palmistry, psychometry, spiritism, telepathy, telekenesis, amongst them. For each of these arts, considerable claims are made by their respective professors. And to each of them, some considerable measure of obloquy pertains. For it must be admitted that in very many cases the claims of their exponents have, upon examination, been found to be largely backed by deception. Trickery and fraud have, in fact, become closely associated with the practice of the so-called occult arts. To very many, to-day, the terms occultism and the occult arts connote chicanery on the one side, and delusion on the part of

12

those who profess to believe in the claims made.

Now nothing is more certain than that, from remote antiquity, there has been a belief in a widespread practice of mysterious arts. Demonology and divination, sorcery and necromancy have been believed in as occult arts from the dawn of history. The oldest documents, the most ancient monuments, tradition, mythology, and folklore, all bear witness to a belief in the practice of secret arts. It would appear, then, that from the oldest transmitted oral repetitions, which crystallised later into folklore, as well as from the records and monuments of the most extreme past, it may be established that it was a constant subject of belief that subtle and mysterious powers existed, and that there were also always those who claimed to be able to use them.

It has been inferred above that certain arts now thoroughly understood and widely practised, were at one time regarded with awe and suspicion, as occult and secret arts. They have now passed their test successfully, and have established themselves firmly as true arts of unblemished reputation and indisputable usefulness. In this little work, it is proposed to examine the claims of several of the alleged arts which are still in the outer darkness. They are still discredited, because their practice has been frequently found to be partly or wholly supported by deception. It is thought possible by the writer to give reasonable grounds, of a sound scientific character, for the basis of these claims. It is hoped to demonstrate that these occult arts may in time, perhaps in the near future, be admitted into the company, on equal terms, of their collateral relatives.

Ten of the occult arts are chosen for the purpose, viz., alchemy, astrology, clairvoyance, psychometry, spiritism, telepathy, hypnotism, geomancy, palmistry, and divination by omens and oracles. Each, distinct in itself, has a common basis, so that there is a natural continuity for the series. Though interacting, they are not mutually interdependent. The failure to establish one or more as a real art does not therefore necessarily invalidate the demonstration of the others. Throughout the work an attempt has been made to use simple language and to avoid the use of technical terms. At the same time, it must be obvious that the analysis of such subjects must require accurate definition which is only to be made by the use of suitable terms. The sequence taken in the chapters is not altogether an arbitrary one.

That the world grows rapidly vastly richer in knowledge is indisputable. And as its accumulation of carefully observed and recorded facts becomes greater, and its classification of them more scrupulously accurate, the hopelessly unpractical hypothesis, nay the impossible speculation, of yesterday becomes the commonplace reality of to-day. In no field has scientific investigation received more ample reward than in that of the physical sciences. Here discovery has succeeded discovery with almost alarming celerity during the last quarter of a century, and this without violent reversal of existing theories. It has been rather an extension of view, widening the range, while at the same time filling in the gaps left in the earlier conceptions. Then, too, there has been a more complete apprehension of the details of the vast body of knowledge which were but indifferently perceived before.

In physics, to give an example, the progress

made in recent years has been unparalleled. The names of a small group of pioneers stand out prominently, each the conqueror of a fresh stage. Ramsay, Lodge, Crookes, Thompson, Becquerel, Rutherford, Soddy, Elster and Geitel all have contributed their quota to the common fund, by years of painstaking research in contiguous fields of study. In every case we have a mass of facts experimentally obtained, and these statements of fact, though not easily verifiable by the layman, may unhesitatingly be believed. We shall refer presently, at length, to some of these discoveries, and it is therefore well to make this point clear, so that there may be no confounding " a statement of fact " with a mere speculation.

It has very frequently happened that the verification of a " fact," demonstrated again and again with scientific exactitude, has been foreshadowed by the speculation of the more daring thinkers of a previous age. Unknown elements have been suggested as necessary to complete the scheme of the periodical classification, and in due time the discovery has occurred of that particular " element " with its predetermined characteristics, all of

16

which have been accurately forecasted. It then falls naturally into its place in the scheme.

Radium itself was a typical element of this kind—its discovery having been predicted by the necessity for filling in the gap between its nearest neighbours, above and below, in the table of the elements. It will be, however, mainly with demonstrated facts that we shall deal here, though it may be desirable to refer to theories arising from them. The theories these workers advance, based upon these facts, are credible inasmuch as they explain the phenomena observed. By the light of increased knowledge, these theories may be, as precedent ones have been, expanded and modified to cover a wider body of ascertained fact; but such as they now are, we may accept them as the work, in every case, of one entitled to speak with authority. And both the facts presented, and the theories resulting therefrom, point in one direction : the truth of the old-world dictum of the alchemist.

" There abides in nature a certain form of matter which, being discovered and brought by art to perfection, converts to itself all imperfect bodies that it touches." So said

the ancient alchemist, and from this pro-
position, and the effort to substantiate it in
fact, centuries of ill-rewarded toil supervened.

" In chemistry we recognise how changes
take place in combination of the unchanging."
This is the verdict of modern chemistry, the
natural successor of alchemy.

In each case it will be noted there is the
postulate of an essential element of simplicity
and perfection upon which the more transitory
forms of matter depend. And modern research tends ever in this direction: to
establish more certainly the homogeneity of
matter; its oneness in essence. It is by
presenting a simple exposition of these recent
discoveries in chemistry that it is hoped to
shew that there is a sound physical basis for
alchemy viewed by the light of modern
science. And further, that the derided quest
of the universal solvent was no mere dream,
but rather an intelligent, if imaginative, forecast of a fact now practically demonstrated.

Alchemy is dealt with first, because in any
analyses we must work from the best-known
to the less well-known. The basis of our
knowledge is derived from the evidence of
our senses. Sensation begins with the

18

physical world. In the world of physics, of chemistry in short, we begin our acquaintance with the occult arts. Astrology naturally follows because of the physical relationship between the other celestial bodies and our own, and their physical, and subsequently determined psychical, influences upon our globe and upon ourselves. Closely associated with the higher degrees of sensation are psychometry and clairvoyance, dependent upon psychic senses which, it will be demonstrated, are latent in most of us, and active in some. These psychic senses are passive, inasmuch as they receive impressions only.

Telepathy—human wireless telegraphy—follows. This is dependent upon a psychic sense and a power—latent in most of us—of transmitting messages. Spiritism or necromancy continues the series, as an application and extension of the principles laid down in the earlier chapters. Then follow the four others. Hypnotism shews the obedience of the physical body to the externally expressed will and idea of another. It illustrates also the functions of telepathy, clairvoyance and clairaudience exhibited by the normal individual when the normal faculties are inhibited. Palmistry is used to shew the correspondence of form of the instrument with the uses to which it is allied. Omens are shewn to be the indications of a future event which the present outlines and determines.

A final chapter concludes the series, with a brief summary of the general conclusions which it is believed have been logically demonstrated.

CHAPTER II

ALCHEMY

WHAT is alchemy ? And who were the alchemists ? These two questions naturally precede an inquiry of this kind. According to some, alchemy was the early form of chemistry ; its object, the supposititious art of making gold and silver from the baser metals. Its dominant theory was that any of them, lead for example, contained the same constituents as gold mixed with impurities. To effect the transmutation all that was necessary was to remove the impurities by the philosopher's stone. The great quest, therefore, was for this alkahest, or universal solvent. And, yet later, when the adepts had attained some knowledge of physiology and drugs, to this was added the search for the " magisterium " which, in addition to transmutation, would also heal all diseases. Then finally came the search for the " elixir vitæ " by which human life should be indefinitely prolonged.

That metals were compounds of mercury, sulphur and salt, and that by altering the proportions of the ingredients a new metal might be formed, were also the " popular " ideas of historical alchemy. It is believed that the pseudo-historical personage, Hermes Trismegistus (we still give the popular view, on which we comment later) was the earliest and principal alchemist. The term "hermetic" is obviously derived from this character. Of the early alchemists, outside their own craft, little is known, and we pass therefore, still adhering to the popular accounts, to the historical period.

Geber, an Arabian, first introduced the study of alchemy into Europe. Then next, in comparative importance, came Albertus Magnus, a German Dominican friar of the thirteenth century, and Lully and Roger Bacon of the same epoch. The latter, though a keen alchemist, was an opponent of necromancy and magic. The following century saw a great increase in the practice of alchemy, and in England an Act of Henry IV.

was passed declaring attempted transmutation a felony. But in spite of opposition and persecution, the study was pursued in successive centuries.

Paracelsus (Von Hohenheim), in the early sixteenth century, was a prominent alchemist, though a lecturer on medicine at the University of Basle; Johann Thölde, in the seventeenth century, and Dr Price, England, of the late eighteenth century, bring the records of its continuity as a " science " down to a near historical era. It is avowed also that there are at least three secret societies in existence to-day whose object is a continuance of the work of the alchemists on a quasi-religious basis. The popular view has, however, never varied, and it has always been the custom amongst the majority to deride alchemy and its claims, though many famous names have been identified with it. So much for the views presented by the uninitiated.

Alchemy has, however, its devotees to-day, and these should be heard in their own cause. " Alchemy " is an Arabian term, or rather an Arabianised form of the Greek " chemica "— its Eastern representation being " ul-khemi " or "al-kimia." Another derivation of "alchemy" is "Al" or "El" (Hebrew), the deity name, commonly translated "God," meaning "mighty" or "supreme," and "chemi" "fire": or the God and patriarch "Kham," also the name of Egypt.

The hermetic philosophy, which is largely the foundation of alchemy, was named after Hermes Trismegistus, the Grecian appellation of the thrice-great Hermes, the Egyptian. Hermes actually is the generic name of many writers of ancient Greece on philosophy and alchemy. His Egyptian prototype was the god Thoth or Thot. As Hermes-Thoth-Aah he is the Thoth, whose bright side of the moon is supposed to contain the essence of creative wisdom. As the serpent, Hermes-Thoth is the divine creative wisdom. It is thus seen that the earliest work of the hermetic philosophers was the pursuit of wisdom, as both the Egyptian Thot and the Greek Hermes were, in each land, respectively the deity of wisdom.

Dr Wynn Westcott, an eminent authority on Freemasonry, archaic symbolism and occult lore, says that " the earliest use of the actual term ' alchemy ' is found in the work of

Julius Firmicus Maternus, who lived in the days of Constantine the Great. The Imperial Library in Paris contains the oldest extant alchemic treatise known in Europe : it was written by Zosimus the Panopolite about 400 A.D. in the Greek language ; the next oldest is by Æneas Gazeus, 480 A.D.'' This refers to existing documents and takes no account of older works destroyed, or maintained secretly.

Democritus of Abdera was an alchemist, and to him may be credited in historical times the atomic theory of matter more recently restated by Dalton. The introduction into Europe generally of the study of alchemy came through Geber, the great Arabian sage and philosopher of the eighth century, though from papyri and other documents now known as hermetic treatises, it is evident that alchemy was practised in Egypt and China from the first dawn of civilisation in these remote empires. Kings and priests were its students, and it is held that its beginning as a science antedates the construction in astronomy of the zodiacal systems.

Much of the alchemic literature was probably written, if not in fact all of it, in the language of symbolism. Thus what was to the profane merely the arbitrary conception of matter as composed of sulphur, mercury and salt, typified to the initiated the three aspects of the divine science. For alchemy was concerned with Cosmic, human and terrestrial evolution, and these were represented on the physical plane by the trinity of mercury, sulphur and salt. The transmutation of metals was only the material concept of one phase of the archaic philosophy. The alchemists intuitively grasped the vital truth of the one homogeneous substance from which all grosser manifestations of matter arose, and sought to reduce the composite bodies, with which they experimented, to that primal base, and, by regrouping it, to attain the production of the noblest element.

On the higher planes of thought it was, and is, their purpose to sublime the grosser nature of man, represented by his material body, and effect the spiritual alchemy by which that body should triumph over death and become immortal. And this is the purpose of those secret societies to which reference has been made. Silently, but steadily, they are pressing back the boundaries of the physical body and opening to the world the possibilities of a real immortality, without the intervening loss of consciousness —the transposition of the " ego " to other planes of existence without the snapping of the silver cord.

But the purpose of this work is not so much to argue the reasonableness of these exalted claims as to urge the truth of the probability of material alchemy—the transmutation of metals by purely physical means, and according to the theories of modern science. If we can prove by the recent researches that it may be considered demonstrated that there is but one universal substratum for material phenomena, and that matter itself is but a transitory form of an underlying power of manifestation, then it must be obvious that transmutation is at least possible, though perhaps not an accomplished fact, and we shall have done what we set out to do.

Incidentally, of course, it will be proved that alchemy was always on the right road, though the methods of its professors may at times have been irregular and even in instances have savoured of quackery.

It is desired to present the case as simply as possible, but it will be necessary to deal with matters which, though neither mysterious nor abstruse, are yet possibly not within the normal range of the ordinary individual; and because of this, care will be taken to err on the right side of simplicity and explanation, rather than to leave points unexplained which may already be known.

But first of all, we must render to alchemy the meed of appreciation which is now so fully recognised as its due by its mighty daughter chemistry. For taking once more the popular view, it is seen that it was the hope of the alchemists, in one aspect of their studies, that a chemical combination of metallic bases and alloys, sublimed and distilled by heat and powerful reagents, would result in the production of virgin gold. Careful records were kept of the processes employed, as it was hoped, when a successful essay had been made, to simplify the operations, and in time discover the means of the " direct transmutation " of any of the metals into pure gold.

In the same way, by the admixture of the vital essences of rare drugs and herbs, known to have high medicinal powers, they trusted to distil the " water of life "—a potion so efficacious that a few drops, taken occasionally, would serve to arrest the decay of the tissues and nervous systems, and maintain the vital principle in a frame which would retain continual vigour and virility.

The pursuit of " knowledge " was the inspiring cause of their efforts. In order to acquire all that they desired of wisdom, one short earth life-period was quite inadequate, and an existence prolonged for centuries, with unimpaired intellectual power and without decadence of the physical system, was but the means to an end. The possession of unlimited wealth, to be provided by the ability to produce as much gold as was desired, was essential to permit them to devote all their time to study. It would also have enabled them to provide the costly and numerous instruments and materials required for research. Travel, also, would have been desirable; boundless riches would thus have expedited, and simplified, all arrangements necessary for a closer acquaintance with men and things.

In the interim, out of the obscure research after the apparently unattainable, born of wearying labour and heart-burning failures, chemistry arose triumphant. It was a precocious reproduction of its foster parent alchemy. Fruitless experimenting—fruitless so far as the original object was concerned—was pregnant with great results for its offspring. A sturdy child, this infant, which, well nourished with the patient observations of its parent, thrived beyond expectation and comparison.

For decades — we had almost written centuries—the sciences were studied concurrently. The earnest student did not easily drop the creed of ages. Gradually, though, the separation between parent and child became more pronounced, and with the greater knowledge which was acquired of the laws of combination, dissociation and proportion, the search for the " alkahest," although not absolutely abandoned, was put aside for the wonders of the more extensive field of analytical chemistry.

Empiricism, progress by experimental research, in due time gave place to speculative hypothesis. Hypothesis, and the resulting theories, were again subjected to rigorous

30

tést, and retest, to verify their consistency by further experimental examination. And so the mighty infant rose in dignity to become an " exact science " in strict proportion to the relegation of its parent to the limbo of a partially forgotten past.

Whilst the " atom " of Democritus and Dalton, the philosophers whose work was separated by two millenniums, has on the one hand been broken down into corpuscles and ions, the atoms, in obedience to the laws the philosophers jointly discovered and stated, have been used, synthetically, to build up, to create in fact, bodies which are new to Nature's own processes. The atoms are, in fact, the bricks with which the chemist builds his houses, and as the laws of association of the grosser particles are now fairly well known, the chemist wields his magic to produce new composite bodies, by synthesis, with comparative ease. Month by month the number of new compounds artificially created rises by leaps and bounds.

But analytical chemistry has, in the past few years, made more wondrous advances. To Madame Curie must be assigned the honour of demonstrating to an astounded world that new property of matter which we call " radio-activity." The path to this surprising discovery had been paved by the investigations of Crookes in the cathode rays, followed soon after by the further observations of Lenard and Röntgen.

Later came the discovery of the S and N Rays, viz. those successively named after their observers, Niewenglowski and Becquerel. Most of these discoveries were bound up and associated with the phenomena of Röntgen Rays, and their mysterious properties in affecting photographic plates, and the penetration by the rays of what had hitherto been considered impenetrable matter. These phenomena were generally those of the ultra violet rays of the spectrum produced electrically in vacuum and otherwise.

Another line of research was, however, attracting considerable attention. This was the phenomena of phosphorescence and the absorption of light and its subsequent emission by variously active bodies. Becquerel, however, determined to get beyond the production of a ray due to the absorption of sunlight in the material with which he experimented. Many were the different substances

32

he tried, amongst others being that of uranium. This yielded its secret. For without exposure to light, it affected the isolated and unexposed photographic plate, in close proximity to which it was placed for some time in the dark.

Becquerel himself says, " I recognise that the emission of the rays was produced spontaneously even when the substance had been kept completely sheltered from any previous exposure to light." This, then, proved that the emission of rays was due to an inherent property of the substance itself, which appeared to manufacture them.

Two observers of Becquerel's researches, Monsieur and Madame Curie, speculated as to the possibility of this property being due to the impurities in the uranium itself. They accordingly experimented with pitch-blende, the parent substance from which uranium was obtained. Some specimens of pitch-blende, they discovered, were many times more radio-active than even metallic uranium. The inference was obvious : some unknown substance was contained in the pitch-blende other than uranium, or other simple, known bodies, which gave rise to the phenomena of

3

radio-activity, and to discover this all their energies were bent.

Step by step they dissociated in turn each of the constituents of pitch-blende, until they had obtained a residue which was one hundred thousand times as active as uranium. This substance was not the element radium, but compounds formed with it by bromine and chlorine. For radium itself had not been isolated. As has been said, it was Madame Curie who achieved the final triumph of obtaining chemically pure radium, which, when isolated, was found to exhibit one million three hundred thousand times the radio-activity of the uranium which led to its discovery.

Without going too closely into technical details, we may consider this property of radio-activity to be exhibited by the gradual dispersion of infinitely minute particles of its substance flying off into space. These radiations of substance have been found to divide naturally into three quite distinct classes, and are alluded to as the Alpha, Beta and Gamma Rays. A portion of them correspond to the ethereal vibration of the X-Rays, a part to the positive ions given off by glowing incandescent bodies, and a portion of them have been proved to be corpuscles. The Alpha and Beta Rays we do not need to examine closely for our present purpose, which is more dependent upon the nature and properties of the corpuscles.

These corpuscles are ultimately found to be moving units of negative electricity, and the portions of ether with which they are associated, as the object of physical research. Radio-activity, however, is a property of matter, and, differing in degree only, this property is now known to be exhibited by all matter. Radio-activity, under certain conditions, gives rise to the dissociation and at times to a reconstruction of the ultimate particles of which matter is composed, and the emergence physically of a new condition or form of matter.

Dalton's atomic theory still holds its ground as the basis of chemical change in the laws of affinity and valency, but the hitherto indivisible atom has been found to be a complex structure of more minute particles, in a state of greater or lesser degree of equilibrium, which are not " matter " at all in the ordinary acceptance of the term. These

35

corpuscles, though in no sense material, that is, they do not comply with the fundamental laws of matter, are, however, the basis of matter, and, so far as has been determined experimentally, are all identical in essence whatever their substance or derivation.

Many elements, in fact most of them, are still irresoluble, and it might be thought straining a point to erect upon the phenomena of radio-activity, associated very extensively with a newly discovered element, a hypothesis to cover the whole field of the chemical elements, and their evolution from one homogeneous substance, were it not for an independent line of research.

Spectroscopic analysis and astro-thermometry have enabled us to construct out of a mass of data certain well-defined conclusions: that the stars in their inorganic evolution may be divided approximately into three great classes, of highest temperature, medium temperature, and lowest temperature, and that the highest temperature stars reveal by spectroscopic examination practically only one element as we know it, hydrogen, though in the constitution of these hottest stars there exists what, for lack of a better name, have been termed proto-elements, elements in a state of flux, giving characteristic but feeble indications only of what they will ultimately become upon a lowering of the temperature. And, precisely as we see in organic evolution the simplest types of primordial life-structures evolve successively into higher, or more complex types, so in stellar evolution we are enabled to trace the progressive emergence of element after element in an immutable order.

In each star, as the temperature drops from higher to lower, we find certain of the proto-elements disappear, and the elements, as known under terrestrial conditions, make their appearance in due course. It is also significant that these elements appear in the order in which, by chemical interaction, they become necessary to form the basis of the substratum requisite for the exhibition of physical life. This point, however, will be dealt with more fully in a future chapter. At present, we are more concerned with the striking testimony afforded that at the earliest demonstrable stage of evolution the material universe is practically composed of but one element, and that the lightest of them all.

This is one of the " facts " for which

37

important consideration is claimed. The hottest stars are the earliest demonstrable worlds, for everywhere we see the attempt to balance the temperature by exchange of heat, with a reduction from the relatively high temperature of an object to the relatively low temperature which succeeds it. We omit for the moment the manner of the formation of the star masses, and deal with them as we find them. These hot stars, then, are the earliest, and they are composed of but one element, hydrogen.

This gas possesses many remarkable properties, chief of which is its wonderful lightness; it is, in fact, the lightest known " material " substance, and it was imagined at one time that it was the parent substance from which all other elements were to be derived. This has been proved to be a fallacy, for hydrogen is an element, and the atom of hydrogen is itself resolvable into its constituent particles. It is, however, a gas so light that it has been stated on authority that our earth exhibits insufficient gravitative power to hold the molecules of this gas attracted to it. In other words, that hydrogen, in a free state, could not exist on the surface of this globe, but by its own kinetic energy would fly off into space. This gives some idea of the minute size of the hydrogen atom and its immense activity.

But the hydrogen atom is conceived to be one thousand times the mass of the corpuscle, which forms its etheric substance. The single atom of hydrogen may therefore be composed of a thousand corpuscles. As it has happily been expressed, " Matter is an aggregation of X molecules : a molecule is an aggregation of Y atoms, and an atom is a structure of Z corpuscles."

The corpuscle, by analysis, is a moving unit of electricity associated with a modicum of ether, and ether, so far as science has been able to determine, is apparently a homogeneous, indivisible, structureless, infinitely-extensive, space-filling medium. What precisely ether *is,* and what precisely electricity *is,* we cannot at present definitely say. The most we can with certainty state is that if there be anything at all which has tangible— as opposed to merely phenomenal—existence, it is this duality of substance and motion : the *medium* ether and the *energy* which agitates it.

It has been customary until recently to speak of "matter and motion" as the ultimate components of the universe, but the definition has been expanded and we must now substitute "ether" for matter. As the earlier and ruder conceptions of the ancients, that the elements were "air," "earth," "fire," and "water," gave way in turn to the periodic classification of nearly eighty "elements," so in turn we see the resolution of the diverse "elements" into the parent substance "ether."

Striking similarities in the "groupings" of the elements had paved the way for this. Many of the elements were so closely correlated in physical characteristics that it seemed reasonable to assume that they were but differing arrangements in ultimate structure of the same material, or substance, and this speculation has now passed into a theory which receives strong and authoritative support. The whole universe in its kaleidoscopic manifestations may be reduced "materially" to its one primeval homogeneous substance, ether, the impalpable, imponderable space-pervading medium (which evades any recognition by the physical senses), and to electricity, its twin-soul, the energy which demonstrates itself and its medium to us physically.

Granting the accuracy of these propositions, electricity may be conceived as the universal solvent or alkahest—the hidden spirit of nature which can resolve all material aggregations into their own primal substance and can reconstruct that " substance " into any alternative form or condition desired. It may, by loosening the bonds of cohesion, affinity and polarity, reduce the gross material body of the elemental dross, lead, into its pure and primordial anti-type etheric substance, and, by a re-association, by the laws which govern the functioning of that substance, emerge once more into material being as virgin gold.

Electricity again may be regarded as the " magisterium magnum " or elixir of life. For, as the vital factor which underlies the chemical action of metabolism, it is essentially the energy which produces the changes and gives rise to the physical phenomena which we apprehend as the functioning of life in organic matter. It is another form of the energy we see in radio-activity.

To sum up, we think we have been able to shew that the cult of alchemy was founded upon two great propositions which have now received substantial demonstration, (a) the underlying unity of substance and interchangeability of " material form " and contingent properties, and (b) the conservation of energy. The ancients doubtless did not phrase it so, but this was merely due to the limitation imposed upon their expression by lack of development. Intuitively they had sensed these two eternal verities and formulated them to the best of their ability : crudely, perhaps, when viewed by the later niceties of scientific definition, but none the less sanely and surely.

CHAPTER III

ASTROLOGY

ASTROLOGY is the reputed art by which, it is alleged, a forecast may be made of the principal events which will happen in the life of any individual whose birth date and hour are known. The celestial bodies are held to have definitely directing influences upon the career, which is shaped for good or evil, as the preponderating influences of the stars or planets are beneficially, or detrimentally, opposed or aggregated.

Man must have recognised quite early in his progress as a reflecting organism that he was surrounded by great forces against which he struggled in vain. He saw that he was almost powerless to control or direct the course through which he moves. He was always the subject of his environment. His greatest achievement could be brought to nought by the most trivial happening of natural forces. Without the knowledge of the sciences, which civilisation brings, he could only grope on blindly, without the conviction borne in upon us that everything follows the action of immutable laws. We know that there is neither accident nor chance. We are assured that there is only cause and effect.

But man would naturally endeavour, when he first began to use his reflecting powers and reasoning, to try to assign a cause for what he observed. His ideas were not always sound. A personality was assumed for the forces of nature. There were good spirits and bad spirits who animated these forces. The sun, the apparent cause of light and life, was good. The lightning and the hurricane, which destroyed things, were the expression of evil spirits. They were to be appeased, while the good spirits were to be honoured and adored. In prehistoric times, when marching or hunting by night, man must have been impressed by the glowing stars above him. His mind must have demanded their uses and purpose.

He had already perhaps noted the differences in the tides and their correspondence with alterations in the appearances of the moon. The appearance of a comet in the skies would almost naturally be coupled with any coincident great events of an unusual character.

But the stars themselves would undoubtedly be the cause of his most earnest questions. Compared with the transient things of the earth their very imperviousness to change would impress him profoundly. Their mystic arrangements in the heavens, outlining to his imagination the glorious contours of his eternal gods and goddesses, would cause heart-searchings as to their influences upon man and the earth.

From repeated and continual observation, the courses of the planets were noted and recorded, and in due time their conjunctions and oppositions were used to explain inferentially the more extraordinary happenings to those in high places. Whatever occurred had to be explained somehow. And in those remote times the most widely separated events were held to be connected if this would favour a solution of the problem. The appearance of a comet would be assigned as the cause of a famine, or an earthquake be attributed to a period of exceptionally severe weather.

There can be little doubt that the first beginnings of astrology had their rise in this manner. But these rude records of elementary meteorology would in time be succeeded by more exact observations of the stars. And so in course of ages the science of astronomy itself had its origin. But astronomy—the record of the star motions—would always be of less importance then than the significance attached to such motions. Whilst man still lacked a comprehensive general explanation or theory of the universe, the greatest scope for the powers of the imagination lay in astrology. There would have been thus two great schools—the observers and the interpreters. One would have been occupied almost wholly with the material sides of masses and motions, and the other with the specific influences which they exercised.

Astrology, then, undoubtedly had its origin in a comparison of striking phenomena which were observed to occur simultaneously with certain conjunctions or oppositions of the stars. The most learned men at Court were undoubtedly those who possessed a knowledge

46

of star motions. It was a courtier-like act which prompted the comparison of the king with one of the heavenly bodies. From this to the association of the idea of their connection was an immediate step, when coupled with great incidents occurring with changes in the position of the stars. When the data, which resulted from close observation extending over long ages, had been carefully classified in their relations to the events, certain well-defined characteristics were assigned to each of the more prominent heavenly bodies. The sun, moon and planets, owing to their proximity to our globe, were assumed to exercise a greater influence over the destiny of the individual concerned, and their specific influences were calculated with much greater precision and accuracy of detail.

As time progressed, so the observed influences were more definitely settled, and a science arose which presumed to portray distinctly the chief events of the life. Some of the planets had baleful influences, some beneficent, and accordingly as they were observed at the moment of birth to have occupied certain relative positions, so was the course of the life satisfactory or unsatisfactory.

47

As the motions of the celestial bodies were constantly varying their relative positions, owing to the differences in their orbits and rates of speed, so their influences were reputed to affect variously the course of the life under consideration. The conjunction of two maleficent bodies resulted in a direful crisis, whilst the opposition of a good planet to a bad one neutralised the danger. Similarly, two good planets in conjunction produced particularly good omens, which might be expected to result in unprecedented good fortune. It was entirely a question of balance of " forces." And as these were constantly varying, they were held to account for every possible combination of circumstances.

In the Near East, from the earliest dawn of history, astrology was a venerated science. The Chaldeans spread it through Babylonia and Egypt, and later Greece and Rome, and so to our own medieval civilisation. The Far East, too, was always deeply concerned with astrology. China in her oldest universities had chairs of astrology. In the mid-East also, in Arabia and Persia, astrology was honoured from time immemorial. Princes and great generals in all affairs of importance consulted the astrologers to determine how far the stars would aid or defeat the ends of their enterprises.

Horoscopes, which set forth the nativity—the course of the life, and its principal events—were thus prepared. The birth moment being known, that point of the ecliptic was marked which rose above the horizon at that time. This gave the mode of division of the zodiacal signs into houses. Each of the houses was assumed to have influences particularly over various parts of the body alternatively with the affairs of the individual concerned. To quote from a popular work on astrology—" The seventh house has dominion over marriage contracts, agreements, partners and matters of exchange. In the body it has relation to the loins and kidneys." Further—" It has been ascertained beyond all doubt or cavil that the ruling of the ancients in this matter is altogether reliable, however empirical it may appear." It might be thought, perhaps, that "hypothetical" would be a better word to employ than " empirical."

Positions and motions of the sun, moon, stars and planets through the houses at the birth moment modified the general signi-

4

ficance of each. It was, of course, only by the most careful calculation that the effect of such modification could be represented. The general inferences were susceptible to emphasis or limitation according to the accuracy of the calculations, and these would not only account for the varied incidents of each nativity, but the grossest errors might be explained by failure to employ precision in the aspects.

It is not desirable here to go into explicit details of the alleged science. It is sufficient for the purpose to establish that it was founded on exact knowledge and observed data. Moreover, it had its satisfied adherents in all ages and all climes, as indeed it has yet. A short historical sketch may be permitted to introduce its principal exponents. Perhaps the greatest astrologer of ancient times was Berosus, of whom it is said that nearly all his prophecies were fulfilled. It may have been, as it is urged, that his acquaintance with the ruling powers was such that his prophecies were merely astute conjectures. But this would be insufficient to justify more than a fraction of his prognostications. Firmanus was the great Roman astrologer whose prophecies were associated with the fall of Rome. Caligula, too, it is undeniably recorded, was warned of his death by Sulla. Abumansur was the Arabian astrologer of the ninth century, whilst Nostradamas, in the sixteenth, achieved distinction which carried his name successfully to our own times. In the seventeenth century Morin, who died in Paris, may be considered the last of the illustrious line.

So far for its practical exponents. On the bibliographical side there is an immense amount of material available. Amongst Hindoo classical writers are to be found Garga, Parashara and Mihira. The mythology of Greece teems with astrological allusions in its cosmography. Of the classical writers of Greece who subscribed a belief in the principles of astrology are Aristotle, Hipparchus, Hippocrates and Thales. The name of Ptolemy is associated with the first promulgation of the true astrological science. Firmicus, later, enlarged the observations of Ptolemy.

It has been argued that the recent discoveries of two more important planetary bodies—Uranus and Neptune—must necessarily have destroyed any value that the earlier science possessed. But astrology has its answer ready. It is that each of the planets has its own influence. The newly discovered bodies possess different influences from the others. Further, it is urged that the discovery of yet more planets would not nullify the observed influences, but merely expand them into more definite predictions. The discovery of these two important planets, it is further claimed, have enabled astrologers to fill in the blanks in ancient predictions. Events have occurred which in the most detailed horoscopes were not foreseen. The influences of the then undiscovered planets were ostensibly the cause of the events. Being unknown themselves, they could not be used to predict the specific features to which they gave rise.

In the great renaissance of the middle ages the revulsion, which had been first perceptible among some of the Grecian philosophers, completed the severance between the antique "psychical" science of astrology and its more modern progeny, "physical" astronomy. Generations of painstaking observation, coupled with the increased facilities for exactitude given by the discovery of the telescope as we now know it, combined to place astronomy in the front rank of physical sciences. The comparatively recent discovery of the spectroscope has advanced it yet further, and astrophysics, its latest phase, has enabled us to investigate and classify the material composition of the stars, even the most distant.

The purely " physical " influences of the heavenly bodies upon our globe itself have been admitted for centuries, and the tide of admission grows yearly stronger. Gravitational influences were the admitted outcome of the Newtonian theory, and tide motions on this planet were accredited to this cause. With the more recent advances made in the sciences of magnetism and meteorology we are assured that the sun's influence is definitely responsible for our incessant weather changes. Sunspots produce magnetic storms on the earth, and the abnormal rainfall is attributed to the same source.

More daring are the speculations that assume that earthquakes may be due to particular conjunctions of the nearer heavenly bodies occasioning a greater gravitational stress, at that period, in the thin crust of the globe. A tide motion in the solid, so to speak.

53

But it is to the electrical or magnetic aspect of influences of the sun and other celestial bodies that we turn for a modern justification of astrology. Granting that these influences, of the sun at any rate, do appreciably affect the earth, we have a definite clue to follow. A very close relationship is observed, in most individuals, between the nervous and mental systems, which are affected most intensely by magnetic or electrical stresses. The approach of a thunderstorm is accompanied by nervous, physical and mental derangement. To some temperaments the deprivation of sunlight even, for any continued period, results in physical and mental prostration. There is no question of the virtues of sunlight in the cure of certain diseases. The sceptic may here object that these effects are purely physical. But who will undertake to say where the " physical " ends and the " psychical " begins ? The safest assumption to make is that " physical " and " psychical " effects are in fact identical manifestations, differing in degree rather than in essential nature. Electricity is a mode of motion of which life is another example of more complex mode, apparently.

54

The magnetic storms of the sun which disturb our terrestrial magnetism may well be assumed, under suitable conditions, to be able to disturb the vibration rate we call Life, either to increased rate, which may result in dissociation or death, or to decreased rate, which, in pathological parlance, is translated " loss of tone," or " disease." And such disease may be either physical or mental.

Sun-ray, Röntgen, and " N " Ray treatment are quite the mode now for experimenting with obscure forms of physical derangement and cellular dissociation, and even of mental disabilities. It is hoped to combat the ravages of disease germs by these means. But the germs themselves are " microcosms," worlds in miniature, built by the aggregation of atoms. And the atoms—what are they ? Mere foci of force impulses ; vibrating, rotating force-whirls of matter-ether. Sun-rays, Röntgen, and " N " Rays are undulatory wave motions in the ether. And ether is the foster-parent. Etheric vibration, when acting as Röntgen Rays, etc., is, by the latest dictum of modern science, the most potent " force " to be employed in the disturbance and reorganisation of the complex functions,

55

which in their total aggregate we call Life. If the rays of the sun in sun-bath treatment, and the electrical and magnetic effects of the physician can make the difference, as they undoubtedly do, between health and disease, life and death, who shall say that the astrologer is wholly wrong in principle when he says the same of the uncontrolled actions of the principal heavenly bodies working in unison with, or in opposition to, each other ?

It will be admitted that the future is truly the consequence of the present. They stand in the relation of cause and effect to each other. There is a mechanical sequence always existent between them. The actions of the future are irrevocably bound up with those of the present. Everything follows as an ordered and orderly progression of events. Law rules everywhere. Man physically and psychically does not escape the operation of these laws. Though credited with freedom of action to choose and decide, his every act is conditioned and determined. His emotions, understanding and will are but the expressions of his reactions and reflexes to law.

A man, it is said, is the arbiter of his own destiny. He rules nature. This is a paradox, for it is always nature that rules man. His emotions are essentially the earliest expression of co-ordinated motion obeying the pressures of his environment. His understanding is the result of his experiences with the phenomenal and external world. His judgments— the exercises of his will—are determined by his association of ideas. These determine his course of action as infallibly as they themselves have been impressed upon him as the resultant of external stimuli.

Character, which in man is the relative determinant of his action, is produced by external pressures. We know that this is so, because if we alter the external pressures of his environment man responds accordingly. Our theory of education is based upon the perception of the fact that the mental activities are modifiable by external stimuli. We apply those which experience has led us to believe will produce the characters we desire. But in addition to the efforts consciously directed to produce a suitable character, there are to be considered other external influences which take their part in moulding the character. Amongst these are those referred to above —the etheric stimulations of light, heat and

57

magnetism from the heavenly bodies. These may be assumed to exercise more than a little effect in modifying the other influences met with at times when they are in opposition or in line. And when we examine any given train of events we are always greatly surprised at the trivialities which have immensely altered the obviously necessary sequence. Napoleon, we are told, failed to digest a meal on one occasion. As a result the map of Europe was altered and the world's conqueror was sent to exile. Was it a thunderstorm which affected Napoleon's stomach ? It may have been.

It is the character in every individual which broadly decides his course of life. His general judgments are made in accordance with his character. The man who achieves material success is he who keeps a single idea to the fore and steadfastly pursues it. Psychology is not yet, however, an exact science. We may determine by it, in the abstract, just what course will be followed in given circumstances by a particular individual. In actual life we cannot so forecast, and this is because we are not sufficiently conversant with all the circumstances; nor can we accurately estimate the value of those disturbing factors which may, and do, influence the action of the individual. Circumstances—the environmental pressures—vary from moment to moment and produce a reaction upon the character which modifies its course accordingly. Thus, though we are able to say generally what would be the action followed, this may be varied, indefinably perhaps then, but sufficiently to turn completely in after times the course of the life.

Though astrology may not be wholly justified in its cruder aspect, which would appear to claim an absolute ruling of every incident of the life from the position at birth of the more important celestial bodies, yet when we reflect how subtly a man's character is formed as a result of all the external pressures constantly applied to him, there is reasonable ground for thinking that the stars in their courses do affect him to some very considerable degree. And, finally, it may be said that the astrological readings of horoscopes which have been carefully prepared do actually delineate the principal temperamental and psychological variations of the characters analysed. If this were merely coincidence

—that is, accidental correspondences—the chances are so remote in accordance with the law of probabilities, that there would be very few of such coincidences to be reported. As it is, the general inferences and deductions are in a very high percentage of cases admittedly quite accurate. It may not be clearly explicable why this should be so, but that it is cannot be gainsaid.

CHAPTER IV

PSYCHOMETRY

A MODERN dictionary gives to Psychometry the following meaning:—" The occult power of divining the secret properties of things by mere contact, claimed by some charlatans." This definition will serve if we render its terms somewhat more explicitly. Psychometry, then, is a little known or understood power, claimed by some experimenters in unfamiliar laws of nature, by which not only the secret properties of things may be determined, but by which a train of events associated with an object may be discovered, or interpreted.

To give an example : a psychometrist, to whom has been handed, in a sealed outer cover, a letter, will endeavour to reproduce the emotions which influenced the writer when composing it ; to portray his personality, and the cause which determined his action ; the immediately preceding events connected with the inception of the letter ; and the relationship his personal surroundings bore to current events and persons. The train of " causality " progresses from particulars to universals. Or it may be that a weapon, associated with a crime, is the subject of investigation. It will then be the task of the psychometrist to reconstruct all the details of the crime itself, the motives which were responsible for it, and the determining incidents which led up to its execution. The attempt to demonstrate the probability, or even possibility, of this power may seem futile to the materialist. In attempting the demonstration we will first briefly review the position of modern science in its theory of " force."

"Force is that which changes, or tends to change, a body's state of rest or motion," in its kinetic aspect. There is also the static form in which " passive forces " are postulated. These act independently of motion. A force is said " to do work " actively when changing a body's state of rest or motion, and passively when resisting such changes. Energy is " the capacity for doing work,"

62

of which there are many forms, the principal being chemical, electrical, heat, sound and light. Further, it is stated that if energy in one form is used to do work, the work done, in its turn, produces an equivalent amount of some other energy. For example, if electrical energy be used for chemical dissociation, the work done will again reproduce the energy used in another form, such as sound, light or heat. This is the necessary conclusion of the dogma of the conservation of energy. By the further admission that the ultimate state of matter, as " electrons " or " ions," is probably nothing but static charges of electrical energy, associated with ether, modern science practically admits the conditions necessary for establishing our case for Psychometry. The occultist has his own hypotheses respecting the origin and formation of matter, but as we are more particularly concerned here with " force," we may exclude the nature of matter as inessential to the discussion in which we are engaged.

To make clear the ground it is desirable, however, to re-assert that modern science admits that anything which causes or tends to cause a change in a body's state of rest or motion, is a force. Our purpose here is to demonstrate that thought is a force. Now, some schools of materialistic science somewhat dogmatically state that thought is a function of matter. And matter, they tell us, quite as dogmatically, is essentially inert. That is, matter cannot move of itself. It must be acted upon by a force in order to change its state of rest or motion. The movement of the brain cells, it is said, gives rise to ideation, to thought. The materialist, however, is on the horns of a dilemma. For though he says that thought is a function of matter, before he can obtain thought he has first to posit motion, and his two fundamental postulates are matter and motion. Thought, then, must be correlated with one or the other. The materialist himself would admit that thought is not material. That it is not matter. And if not matter, it must be motion. It cannot be anything else, since, to the materialist there is no other but these two ultimate concepts. If, then, thought is correlated to motion in its aspect as force, it would appear that it is thought which causes the movement of the brain cells, or, more accurately stated

64

perhaps, thought is the movement of the brain cells.

Occultism takes up a definite position. It agrees, broadly, with the postulation of the two fundamental concepts of modern science. It regards the manifested universe as subject to a law of periodicity. There is an out-breathing which culminates in gradations of matter as the outer clothing of gradations of force. The essence of matter and force is one. To our senses, it is manifested as two facets of the one substance. Underlying it as its primal cause are ideation and will. On the physical plane—the normal plane of objectivity—it postulates an ultimate state or condition of matter. This is homogeneous, impalpable and imponderable. None of the properties of matter as we know it are apparent. It would correspond, broadly, to the hypothetical ether of science. But matter to the occultist exists in various planes of objectivity which interpenetrate one another. To the lowest in order is related the material or physical plane of science on which the gross earthly body of muscle, sinew, bone, tissue and flesh functions.

At the termination of a great period of

5

manifestations, an enormous astronomical cycle, the visible universe ceases to exist as a world of objective form. It becomes once more formless and impalpable, returning for a time to its original essence, once more to reawaken to activity. The philosophical conceptions of Spencer in his cosmography are not widely remote from the truth as seen by occultism. Motion is the one reality. It is that which ever is, and was, and will be. It is the ever becoming. And motion denotes life. Life indeed is but a complex of motions : molecular, metabolic, atomic and electric, even to modern science. The latter professes itself unable either to account for the origin of life or to explain its deprivation from some spheres. Occultism postulates life as eternal and infinite. In its highest aspect, life is pure motion. Nothing in the universe, on any plane of action or manifestation, is without motion, and therefore motion or life is the inherent property or quality of matter. There is no dead matter. The atom is instinct with life—with motion. The corpuscles and ions of modern science—the ultimate particles to them—are to occultism worlds in miniature.

66

Motion, then, is life. And thought is motion. Thought, then, is a living force : a moving cause. Thought is that which can change a body's state of rest or motion. Thought causes the motion—it is the motion—of the brain cells. And behind thought lies the will of which motion is the external expression. This is why, then, it is said that to the forces known to physical science, occultism adds another, the most powerful of all. Indeed, in its sublimest aspect, it is the prime cause of all —the " will," of which " thought " is the materialised expression in the phenomenal world.

" Thought," then, is a form of energy, inasmuch as it possesses the capacity to do work. The thought - suggestion of the hypnotist—whether verbally uttered or not— will do work on the subject. In the annals of orthodox science, in the French hospitals, the thought-suggestion has been shewn as " chemical energy " in producing anæsthesia, and in other instances as " heat energy," when a burn—an erosion of living tissue— has resulted from the unuttered thought-suggestion of the operator. Other cases might be cited to demonstrate still further the fact that " thought " is a form of energy, as real as light or electricity.

Thought may well be compared with light, as an undulation of the ether, or to electricity, by virtue of its capacity, as " energy," to create a stress in matter. Like other forms of energy, when it does work, the work will, in its turn, produce an equivalent amount of another form of energy. Light travels in all directions, and with almost inconceivable rapidity. So also does " thought," impressing itself similarly, by its etheric undulations, upon all bodies within its range. When such bodies absorb " thought-energy," work is done by the stress which is created, and this work will reproduce in its turn this, or another form of energy. To return from this necessary lengthy digression to the concrete example. Ideation must precede the will to act. So far as the actions of the writer of the letter, or the perpetrator of the crime, were premeditated, their previous " thoughts " would have been impressed, not only upon the articles specified, but upon every other object within range of their meditations. The thoughts being so impressed, set up a state of stress, and this

68

" work done " has the capacity to produce another form of energy by transformation.

Light, in acting upon a photographic plate, produces a stress which, when suitable means are employed, reproduces itself as chemical energy in dissociation of the silver-salt. Thought being the most vital and energetic of all forms of energy, all bodies are assumed to be more or less amenable to a stress in consequence of its action. It may be assumed that the lapse of considerable time will serve to dissipate this energy by infinitely small gradations of release of the stress. A photograph, fading, in the course of years, may serve as a rough analogy. When the necessary means of transforming the stress is provided, by the presence of the psychometrist, it is suitably released by this " reagent." This may be further explained by reference to the photographic action of light. In this latter art the essentials for the reproduction of a picture are as follows : a sensitive plate, an exposure to concentrated light, by means of a lens, and a reducing agent to render the " latent image " produced by the exposure, visible.

In psychometry, it is held that all bodies

69

are more or less sensitive to thought. That thought, whether conscious or unconscious, acts upon them, as light concentrated upon a sensitive plate does, and produces upon them a " latent image." Their sensitiveness probably depends in a measure upon relative proximity to the locality of the sources of energy, in the same way that the light rays, impressed upon the plate, are those only which are reflected by the objects within the camera's range. The latent image, psychometrically, is made visible or audible, by an agent capable of disturbing the " stress " which occasioned it. The " conscious thought " of the operator acting, like the developer in photography, upon the latent image, transforms the potential or passive energy, into kinetic energy, the energy of motion, *i.e.* sound or light. The etheric vibrations thus released are presented to the inner senses of the psychometrist as " ideation."

This theory also implies that any other object other than those instanced, if present at the time, would enable the psychometrist to reconstruct the scene. A succession of mental pictures is given, in which all that is essential to the reproduction of the events

70

is included, but overlaid and obscured by the other multitudinous impressions associated with the object, which have not yet been dispersed by time. The skilled psychometrist has to dissociate, and delete all other impressions than those essential to the purpose.

So far, one aspect only of psychometry has been dealt with. Another phase of this occult science is the ability to diagnose the properties of bodies, substantially present, but shrouded.

Here again it is urged that nothing but the extended action of natural laws is exhibited. Light, sound and heat are vibrations and undulations, in a scale which apparently exposes numerous "gaps," above, below and between. Gaps to which our normal physical senses fail to respond. These "gaps" are, however, only apparent because the vibrations they represent are inappreciable to us. For example : a sound may either be so low in pitch, or so high, that it is inaudible, but the vibrations are virtually present as "sound" though we do not hear it. So with light. Above and below the series of undulations which are capable of "impressing" our optic nerve are millions of others to which we are insensible. Science, with its instruments of physical research, demonstrates the existence of these " invisible " light rays. The " ions " and " electrons " of the atom of a fragment of gold, or of the atom of carbon contained in a lock of human hair, are in a state of inconceivably rapid rotation and vibration. These vibrations give rise to undulations in the ether. May it not well be that some human organisms possess organs of sense, analogous to our normal physical organs—possibly but an extension of them, or their functions, on another plane of consciousness capable of responding to these more delicate stimuli ? In this hypothesis lies the justification of psychometry, and modern science certainly does more to substantiate than to controvert its claims.

But it may be thought that, though it may be easy to suggest the presence of such senses, it would be difficult to afford any proof of their existence. It is necessary, then, to investigate the principles of man as postulated by occultism. Reference has already been made to the lowest plane of objectivity—the physical plane of modern science—to which is correlated the physical body. Interpenetrating this is what the occultists call the astral or etheric plane. Modern science, in one of its dogmas, says that no two atoms on the psychical plane have ever been in actual contact. If this is so, how does this exact science explain sensation ? What are touch and taste ? It would be difficult, we think, to explain them on the older basis of physics which accepted the atoms as the ultimate particle. But now that modern science believes that matter is not "matter" at all, it comes virtually into line with occultism. For the latter has all along taught that the material particles of science were transient and accidental aggregations of finer substance built into a web of etheric material, so to speak.

It is this web of etheric material which forms the bridge for sensation, which is communicated to the grosser particles of the physical body as stresses. The etheric body, the impalpable and imponderable inner delimiting structure, is the vehicle for receiving, in the first place, the stimuli from outside. This body has its organs of sense corresponding to the objective organs of sense of the physical body. These sense organs are hypothetically postulated, but are demonstrated by dream phenomena, by the subliminal consciousness, and by the hypnotic phenomena. The infallible memory is associated with these sense organs, and the subconscious mind is one of its expressions. Normally these senses do not function for us consciously. That is, our consciousness works only on the lowest plane of all—that of the physical body. In abnormal individuals there is a functioning of sorts on this astral or etheric plane which is semi-conscious only.

In psychometry, these etheric senses are in part awakened. Semi-consciously, sometimes unconsciously, the elementary psychometrist becomes aware of impressions received, he or she does not know whence or even how. But as the faculty is awakened the will stirs the consciousness, which is then carried over to another plane of being and action. It then begins to function as a child does, haphazardly and almost blindly, till it learns by experience to use its newly acquired powers. But there still remains to be acquired the capacity to bring back the knowledge thus obtained.

A rough analogy would be that of the

hypnotised subject. In the hypnotised condition the etheric senses of the subject are stirred by the operator. The subject is seen to be actually conscious on a higher plane of being—on the plane of the sub-conscious mind. But when awakened, the subject is unable to recall the experiences related by himself, for example, to the operator, when in the hypnotised condition. The capacity is not present to bring over on to the ordinary plane of action and consciousness the experiences of the etheric plane. But occultism is in general agreement with the teachings of the laws of evolution. On the physical side it admits the ascent of man from more primitive types. It also postulates a continual ascent for man to a spirithood, and eventually to godhead and omniscience. Further, it lays down most emphatically that there are even now immense differences in mental and spiritual growth. That there are now with us men and women who represent what the general stage of growth mentally and spiritually will be for the race millenniums hence.

It is, then, these etheric senses which will, when they come to be used generally, carry the race forward on another stage of its journey. It will render man practically independent of our three-dimensioned space. It will open out to him records which have been stored etherically and invisibly for him. The impress, the impacts, so to speak, of thoughts upon so-called inanimate objects will be within his range of developments. He will be able, by his astral or etheric senses, to reconstruct the scenes which have passed into the endless cycles of eternity. And he will also be able to construct the future which is the outcome of the law of causation. For the future is contained in the eternal present. There is no dead matter. There are no inanimate objects to the occultist. All is life. All is movement. All is an ever-becoming. Death signifies and connotes changelessness. And there is nothing unchanging. Nothing is imperishable save space, motion and the root.

Modern science agrees with these dicta. For space is inannihilable : motion, the cause of energy, is eternal, and the root, matter in its ultimate aspect, is indestructible. It is only the form of matter and the rate and direction of motion that varies. Form is continually changing. Its change posits motion. And motion is life. Matter, then, as form, is the manifestation of life, and the impact, on all matter, of force, as thought, is the cause of its change of state. The change of state may be, frequently is, only a static change. It needs development to convert it into a kinetic change.

To perceive such changes the finer instruments of the etheric senses are necessary. The power to carry the knowledge thus obtained over to the waking consciousness of the physical plane is obtained by the application of experience precisely as in the realm of any other domain of science. Changes of state, the expansion of a body by the application of heat energy, are only perceptible by the trained operator with the necessary instruments to record and measure such changes. But modern science would not deny that such changes happened because it had not the means to descry them or to record them.

Psychometry is concerned with just such changes. The occultists say such changes take place. They describe the instruments by which such changes are observed. They translate with practical application the bearing of such changes. They do this on lines acceptable to modern science. There is neither transgression nor transcendence of natural law. There is merely an extension of the principle of natural law into a field just beyond the present range of physical science.

Psychometry asks only for an impartial hearing in its own interests. It neither begs for favours nor asks for a packed court. It is conscious of its own strength to withstand the test that science with its own hypotheses can apply to it. But it enforces its demand to be tried. It insists that it cannot be dismissed as an idle chimera, because, forsooth, science cannot measure the length of a thought with a foot-rule, nor weigh it in a balance. Modern science must remember that the spring balance, the gramme weight and the foot-rule, are equally indeterminate in ascertaining atomic weight, the velocity of the alpha-rays, or the physical constituents of light.

CHAPTER V

TELEPATHY

IN the previous chapter reference was made to the etheric senses of man. Impressions were said to be thus obtained by the psychometrist, and brought over to the physical plane as sensations. It will be well, perhaps, here to review briefly the ground already covered. In alchemy the universality and homogeneity of substance were traced. Mother earth, the basis of our own physical form, it was demonstrated, was in essence differing modes of expression of the underlying substance, ether. In astrology, the gravitational and other physical influences of the celestial bodies were correlated to their electrical influences. From this it was inferred that there would also be mental or psychic influences. In psychometry, the argument is carried further. The etheric sub-

79

stratum of the globe and the etheric substratum of man were shewn to be mutually affectable and affected. The so-called inorganic matter of science was held to be capable of liberation and transformation by the etheric senses of man. Now we have to deal with the capacity of man to communicate with man by these same etheric senses and organs. For telepathy is the power of communication of mind to mind without the intervention of the normal channels of correspondence of physical sense impressions, sight and sound.

Years ago there was a vogue of so-called thought-reading. Physical contact was made between operator and subject and a hidden article was located, the operator being guided to the spot by the subject. Various theories were elaborated to account for the success which attended these exhibitions. The usually accepted conclusion was that involuntary muscular action, induced by nerve strain in the subject, indicated to the operator sufficiently clearly the way to go. The nerve strain was, of course, induced by the subject concentrating his thoughts on the object. This thought-reading so-called was, however,

80

of the earth earthy. For it simply substituted for the normal modes, sight and sound, another physical sense, touch. In telepathy we have to deal with the possibility of conveyance of impressions in situations where the use of sight and sound and touch would be equally superseded, if not actually impossible, by reason of the limitations of space. It is evident that direct transmission of thought could transcend spatial limits. For thought is not subject to our physical three-dimensionised plane. It is no more difficult to carry the thought to the further side of the world than to the further side of the room. Indeed, the infinite capacity of the universe is the only limitation of thought, if it has any limits at all.

It will be necessary, in the first place, in analysing a specific instance of telepathy, to make fully plain the meanings of the terms now to be employed. We will define precisely the meaning to be conveyed by the term " mind," and then consider the functions of the mind, and the " faculties " employed in so functioning. The ordinary dictionary definition will serve our purpose for " mind," which is given alternatively as " the understanding," or " the whole spiritual nature of man." By this is clearly implied that part of a man's nature which is not "material." Leaving out of the question the philosophical aspect of immortality or permanence, we will agree to call the "mind" that portion of the man which is not subject to the limitations of our three-dimensionised space. It is that within the man which enables him to "think," to "plan," to "will," to "imagine." Whether thought be a function of "matter," as some materialists have it, or not, does not really affect the issue. Thought is a "function," the doing of something, and the doing of something is clearly the exercise of "force."

Any cause which changes, or tends to change, a body's state of rest or motion, is a force. And whether we think of thought as causing the movement in the brain cells, or of undulations in the ether, as light and electricity do, it is still a force with which we are dealing. The "will" is the supreme faculty of the mind. Thought and imagination its two principal functions. Thought, again, being a force, has the capacity to do work, and the work will produce in its turn an equivalent amount of energy of another form. In thinking the simplest form of energy exhibited is that shewn as chemical energy in " cerebration," dissociation or aggregation, of the physical particles of the brain cells. The energy which is produced by the work done, in this building up, or breaking down process, is given out again as etheric undulations. These, like light, are invisible or inaudible till reflected or refracted. Light itself is an invisible undulation, in an invisible medium. This is proved thus. A beam of light projected into a darkened chamber becomes visible only by the " reflection " from the surfaces of the tiny particles which float in the air. If these particles—in any portion of the path of the beam—be consumed, by the application of a bunsen burner, which has no light flame, a distinct track of " invisible light " will be presented, as darkness. The " thought-undulations " of the ether require, then, a substance capable of reflecting or refracting them to make them become visible or audible. The alternative is used advisedly, because we know that it is possible for energy of one sort to change into energy of another kind or form. Light, heat and sound are but differences in pitch of vibration rate.

We now instance a case in telepathy. A quotation of Shakespeare is to be transmitted. As the transmitter reads the passage his " thought " is consciously or unconsciously at work. To read the passage he must first exercise his will to perceive it, his thought to apprehend, his memory to record it. He cannot himself apprehend what is written without " thinking." The act of thinking causes the brain cells to move (even materialists admit this), and by their action a new form of energy is produced—etheric undulations. These undulations, like those of light, spread in all directions with inconceivable rapidity. They impress all bodies within their range with a " latent image " which can be evoked by psychometry. But they do more. They impress also the brain cells with a " stress " which may or may not be appreciable. If the brain impressed be " sensitised," by conscious preparation of cell-structure (polarised by thought-energy), the immediate transformation of the " stress " is manifested by etheric undulations appreciable by the mind of the " subject," as

84

vividly, as accurately, and as immediately as are the thoughts of his own volition. And, at the séance, what of the brain cells of the audience ? is the cry of the sceptic. Why do they not respond to the " stress " ? Practically because in their case there is no developer to render the latent image perceptible.

In hypnotism, when a subject is put into the trance condition, and a suggestion, postdated so to speak, is given, the subject when aroused will be unconscious of the suggestion itself, or of the time when it is to take effect. That such really occurs there can be no doubt, as the accuracy of the fact has been repeatedly proved. In this case we see an instance of a mind, impressing itself as a thought or command, as " stress " upon the brain cells of another, to act in a certain manner at a certain time. Yet when the sleep is terminated, the subject of it knows nothing. When the time approaches to act, he will, however, act, as if of his own volition, in the manner suggested by the operator. The thought " impressed " has created a stress which, when suitable conditions are provided, will liberate the energy to complete the action.

85

During the hypnosis—induced sleep, it will be noted—the normal functioning of the mind of the subject is inhibited, inactive. The operator imposes his will by thought-suggestion, as the " force " to do. But on recovery no trace of this " imposition " is apparent. It is latent, however, and emerges into actuality later only, when conditions permit the energy, present as a " passive stress," to transform.

In like manner with those present at a séance. The stress is, virtually, imposed upon all equally, by the thoughts of the operator, but it is prevented from re-acting by the normal functioning of the other faculties. Suitable conditions would evoke it, as the " latent image," from an indifferently sensitised plate, confused and blurred, and possibly utterly unrecognisable. In the other case we have instanced there is, instead, a " new plate," freshly " sensitised " for each " impression." And this is developed, fixed and printed, instantaneously, to use the more familiar photographic analogy.

This power of telepathy is one which all of the human race possess *in potentio,* but not developed yet for actual use. In the case of some people constant effort has brightened and polished the faculty to such an extent that it is as " normal " to them as speech is now to the remainder of the species.

Surprising as the last statements may appear, they can easily be demonstrated by simple experiments. To some it will appear so easy to acquire a slight command of this " power " that the only wonderful thing about it will then be that they were not conscious of their ability before. To others, who will make the same experiments without the slightest vestige of success, the proofs must lie in the reasonableness and consistency of the hypothesis. It has been said that this faculty is latent in the vast majority. Its development will depend upon the amount of use to which it is put. On the physical plane we do not expect the " athlete " to develop in a starved and stunted frame ; especially if no effort is made to train. So with the mind and its powers. Will, its supreme faculty, rarely receives conscious training to render it " fit." Thought, the chief function of the mind, is also rarely " exercised," and consciously directed, as it should be. Most of us just " drift " instead of thinking.

The ancient philosophers held that if the will were concentrated with persistence, the subject of its thought might, in time, be made to take objective reality. This is, in effect, what telepathists do, to a lesser degree. The " thoughts " consciously impelled actually take objective reality, visibly or audibly, to the recipient's more finely strung inner senses. It is in this " conscious " direction of the thoughts, and a specially attuned " condition " to receive and reproduce them, that the apparent mystery of telepathy is contained. But in it there is nothing incompatible with the teachings of modern science.

For the more or less perfect transmission of thought, two conditions are imperative. There must be a conscious effort to transmit and a conscious effort to receive. We leave for the moment as a side issue the phenomena of hypnotism, with which we will deal again later on. Instances are constantly recurring, which cannot be explained by coincidence, of unconscious transmission of thought. Two persons in the same room will be affected by the same train of thought, or it may be the same refrain of a melody, and when one gives

88

audible utterance to it, the other will remark, " How strange ! That has been running through my brain." One person will hesitate in speaking for a word that will not come, or in writing for a similar cause. The by-stander will think of the word, but possibly before he utters it, the other has also caught the unconsciously projected etheric vibration. This provides an opportunity for exercise. If one be of active mental disposition it is not difficult always to provide the word. And the test may be made more certain by the transmission of an unsuitable word which will be accepted immediately and unhesitat-ingly and then rejected when reflection has shewn its unsuitability. Such instances are, however, only the first childlike stumbling from the " all fours " position to the erect and down again.

When one has mastered the will sufficiently to concentrate the thought, and consciously to project it, a helping hand may be held out to the recipient whose task is somewhat more difficult. For here the mind has to be rendered blank. The plate has to be sensi-tised, but excluded from the ordinary light rays. Only to those which pass through the lens must it respond. The condition of mental passivity is an extremely difficult one to attain. Much of what passes for thinking is mere drifting. And the very effort of trying not to think carries the untrained mind instantly into shoal water. Yet we can teach ourselves not to think. The mind can be rendered passive to a greater or lesser degree. The mind controls the body always to some extent. The emotions sway and distort the physical frame. Fear, anger and joy will induce complex physical changes in the nervous, muscular, bony and tissue structures of the body. But the emotions can be controlled by the will. The will exerted consciously and constantly and powerfully will make a man almost insusceptible to emotional stresses. Man's mental principle acting through his etheric body can attain almost complete mastery over the physical body.

It is then that the possibility of telepathy becomes apparent as a normal function. The thought transmitted by another awakens the etheric sense of the recipient as the wave oscillation of the marconigram actuates the coherer. The local circuit is closed and the message is materialised in the relay. There is nothing mysterious about it, though to the uninitiated the transmission of aerial telepathy is marvellous. But then, so is the more normal mode of telegraphy to those unacquainted with the elements of electrical science. Telephony itself is even more marvellous. For here we have the dissociating of sound-waves, the conversion of mechanical energy into electrical energy, and its conversion into mechanical energy again. In telepathy there is a similar process. The thought energy becomes cerebration or mechanical energy which gives off electrical energy, etheric undulations, these in turn becoming reconverted into mechanical energy or brain movements in the physical body of the recipient, after having been assimilated, as etheric disturbance, by his astral or etheric sense organs.

Of unconscious transmission of thought there are numberless instances on record. Many of them, it will be noted, occur at the time of grave peril or at the point of death. This is suggestive. At such moments the physical body is almost wholly dormant. The consciousness is being exercised on the etheric or even on the mental plane. The recipients, too, are usually those of highly nervous temperament or of imaginative disposition. This is sometimes used as though it were an argument against the validity of such phenomena. The imagination is confused with fancy, as though the two were identical, instead of being, as they are, as wide asunder as the poles. The imaginative individual lives and acts very much on the higher planes of consciousness. In those higher planes the etheric senses are the vehicle. Susceptibility to etheric disturbances is its distinguishing mark. And the unconscious thought-waves impinge upon and impress such individuals because their consciousness is super-normal.

In hypnotism there is a reversal of these conditions. The subject is insensitive to his own etheric disturbances. His physical body is directly controlled by the operator superseding the subject volition. The passivity of the subject and its obedience to external control carries with it its own incapacity to register what occurs. There has been a forcible ejection of the rightful tenant who cannot be expected to be cognisant of the usurper's actions. As a matter of fact, the

92

subject is cognisant because his own etheric vehicle is necessarily used to affect the physical changes.

But a hypnotic subject usually possesses little power of transmission of consciousness from one plane to the other. That his higher principles—his sub-conscious memory, to use the phrases of *exact* science—do carry over the knowledge of events is proved by the fact that post-suggestion is acted upon. The subject finds it difficult, however, to explain why he does certain things. He merely feels that he must. A triumphant vindication this of the truth of telepathy. The memorised, mental suggestion of the operator is obeyed. And it is obeyed by a recipient who has no knowledge, in his normal consciousness, of such a command having been received.

By suggestion, a habitual drunkard, suffering from a veritable fever disease, his whole cellular system polarised by the continued action of the overstimulation of his vibration rate, may be cured. The almost irresistible craving, ever present when in his normal state, to continue the acceleration, is arrested by the thought of the operator, who dominates the system of the subject and compels it to vibrate to its normal rate again. The operator reacts upon the disturbed vibratory system by a process akin to depolarisation, and restores harmony and health.

As a matter of fact, the modern physician owes much of his success, in his conflict with both mental and physical disorders, to the exercise, consciously or unconsciously, of his thought-suggestion. The patient "feels" that the doctor has the ability to do him good, and the cheerful self-assertiveness of the physician itself is the most powerful assistant he could desire to evoke to aid his drugs.

These, ordinarily, effect their purpose by a stimulation of the organs concerned, in a physical manner ; order resulting from chaos by the expenditure of chemical energy. As, however, there is no appreciable difference between the anæsthesia produced by the thought-suggestion, and by a drug, both causing a similar effect by a mode differing in phase, so also there is no difference in the cure of the drunkard. In the one case the mental energy of the thought-suggestion, and in the other the chemical energy of the drugs, has been responsible for the effect. In the case of the hypnotic anæsthesia the action is

94

palpably through the etheric double. Its intimate relationship with the physical compels the latter to respond, immediately, to its own vibration rate.

Materia medica has its limitations, and so doubtless has hypnotism. An infusion of senna, or tincture of iron (both valuable remedies when correctly employed) would not assist very materially in restoring an amputated limb. Nor would hypnotic suggestion. But it is a logical conclusion, if the premises be admitted, that minor pathological effects, as distinct from those of a surgical character, can be produced or modified, by hypnotic suggestion, in precisely the same manner as would occur if drugs were used instead.

Both the patient and the healer in the practice of Christian Science exhibit an earnest belief in the possibility of being healed, and healing. This is a condition favourable to the concentration of effort so necessary for successful hypnotic treatment. The prayers of the patient induce a condition of passivity or subjectivity, on his part, and the will of the healer is consciously exerted by his own prayers, which practically assume the form of a command, or suggestion. Given ideal conditions, it would appear quite feasible that a case of scarlet fever could be successfully treated in this way. A reduction of temperature could certainly be ensured by suggestion, and, with a modification of diet, the progress of the disease germs subdued, if not actually arrested, immediately, by a further exhibition of hypnotic suggestion. It should be remembered that the disease germs themselves, in common with all other forms of organised life, are resolvable ultimately by introspective analysis into " corpuscular groupings," vibrating with inconceivable rapidity, and amenable to change of rate or grouping by the imposition of differing forces, of which thought energy is one example.

From this brief reference to the phenomena of hypnotism, it will be seen that the active transmission of thought, by a conscious operator, is quite a commonplace. Its reception, too, by the sub-conscious mind, and the physical activity resulting from the latter's receptivity, also calls for little comment. It is when the transmitted thought has to be retranslated, as it were, into ideation that we approach once more the occult art of telepathy. The examples given earlier in this chapter indicate plainly a method of empirical research open to all. Passivity can be cultivated. And soon it is comparatively easy to obtain first-hand evidence that telepathy is no more mysterious or wonderful than writing or speaking. It depends upon vibrations of higher pitch than sound—on those approaching to light waves and electrical waves in frequency.

CHAPTER VI

CLAIRVOYANCE

IN telepathy we carried our argument a stage further than it had previously been advanced. The endeavour was made to substantiate the possibility of the communication of the mind of one individual with another. This was held to be possible by the operation of the etheric sense organs. In clairvoyance we have to deal with the extension of the use of these same etheric senses. For clairvoyance is the power claimed of seeing things outside the range of normal vision. It is proposed to shew that the etheric vision is capable of transcending our three-dimensional space.

Now it is first desirable to review the mode of normal vision. We can thus see how far in accord with similarly ascertained scientific laws the claims of the clairvoyant may be.

Normal vision depends upon the fact that rays of light, which are undulations of the ether, are reflected from the substances upon which they fall. Such rays reflected into space again are focussed by the eye on which, in common with other objects in their path, they strike. The optic nerve is stimulated and the impressions of such stimulus are conveyed to the brain. The etheric undulations are here transformed into vision. That is—we see. How precisely the transformation is effected, from the physical reflex into a mental impression, we do not know. But it is suggested that the etheric double, the astral counterpart of the man, is the medium by which the motion of undulation is converted, or transformed, into and on to a higher plane of consciousness.

Such rays of light as are perceptible to the normal vision, or rather which are capable of stimulating the optic nerve, are only a small section of the almost infinite range of light rays. The eye responds only to the rays of the spectrum. But, above and below it, varying immensely in pitch, or wavelength, and frequency, are others. This is demonstrated by photography and radio-

99

graphy. Heat is molecular motion, light is etheric motion. It may be that electricity is inter-etheric motion. Just as there are sounds too low in pitch and too high in pitch for our normal organs to respond to, so there are etheric vibrations to which our ordinary organs will not, or cannot, respond. But because our ordinary organs fail to identify, or to react to, these vibrations, we are not entitled to say that they do not exist. The same holds with our fundamental notions of weight, of mass, and of opacity and transparency.

Light rays do not penetrate sheets of lead. Light rays do penetrate sheets of glass. This appears commonplace until we examine the statements seriously. Then we find that some light rays do penetrate sheets of lead ; and that sheets of glass are quite opaque to the same rays. The ultra violet rays, or X-rays, are referred to. It is seen, therefore, that if there are light rays which behave in this apparently contradictory and extraordinary manner, there is at least a case for inquiry to be made out for clairvoyance, which claims that things can be seen with other means than that of the ordinary light rays, or by means of the ordinary eyes.

It has usually been the custom, in speaking of clairvoyance, to allude to it as " an alleged power of inner sight." Some psychologists, students of the mental sciences, might tender the familiar phrase " imagination," forgetting that labelling a thing afresh is by no means equivalent to an intelligent explanation of the phenomenon itself, its cause, or the method of its working. Accepting, for the moment, that clairvoyance may be but the result of the exercise of the function of " imagination," we will endeavour to see how far this would justify the claim made for ability to see things not visibly present to the normal senses.

In a previous chapter, Telepathy, allusion was made to the mind of man and its faculties and functions. Taking a stand upon the thesis there laid down, "imagination" is postulated as a function of the mind. The etymology of the word is suggestive and instructive. In its older form, its meaning was " to contrive," " to devise " : the exercise clearly of a power of " creation," or formation. Imagination, then, is a " force " by virtue of its power to do work, even if that work be nothing more than the production of " etheric vibrations " which result from conscious or unconscious " cerebration."

The imagination has often been confused with thought. In reality they are as closely allied as are the positive and negative phases of electricity. As, however, we can treat of the energy of electricity either from its positive side or from its negative side, so also we can view the positive and negative aspects of the mind's energy as manifested in " thought " or " imagination." Thought is " positive." That is, it is so with those who think consciously. With most individuals, what passes for thought is mainly "drift." A mere passive reception, and passing along of " thought currents " which are unconsciously " inspired " and " respired."

By the constant " materialisations " of his thoughts, the real thinker, on the other hand, gives proof of the positive character of his thinking, which is merely a fore-shadowing of his future. Imagination is the passive phase of the mind's faculty, which, collectively with thought, is rendered as intellect. Unfortunately, owing to the de-

102

fective " instruction " which passes for education, the power of the imagination is restrained almost to the point of atrophy. Little effort, or none at all, is made to stimulate this indifferently comprehended power. In children, the exercise of " imagination " is constantly in evidence, but as the wrappings of this outer, gross life of flesh are overlaid, its sensitiveness wanes. Wordsworth has finely expressed this in his "Ode to Immortality."

It is to the hyper-sensitive mind of him who communes with nature, laying aside the grosser sensation of the physical life, that this " inner light " is permitted. In the world of art it rules supreme and absolute. The " inspiration " of the musician, the painter or the sculptor, is no more, and no less, than the exercise of a sense which enables them to hear, and see, the " music of the spheres," and the beauties of the " world of visions." To the musician, or to the painter, the theme and the composition are as veritably present " to the eye of the mind " as are the objective realities of the " score " and the " picture " to the normal senses of their beholders. The faculty which art uses to obtain its inspirations is a mere " browsing " in the inner thought-world, a world which in occultism is spoken of as the Astral Light.

This astral light has been described as " an inner, ambient, penetrative atmosphere, a luminous etheric substance, a natural agent of infinite potency." It is as necessary to the " psychic " life of man as atmospheric air is to his physical body. Deprived of either, he becomes " psychically " or " physically " dead. The astral light holds in its bosom electric and magnetic forces, and the germs of every conceivable substance. It is this enveloping " psychic " thought atmosphere, in which are presented the past, present and future as one eternal, ever-present NOW. We cannot separate, even in thought, cause and effect. The "present" is but the result of the " past," and equally so is it true that the "future" is held contained *in potentio* in the "present." When, by the exercise of the imagination, we become cognisant of this vast storehouse, the mind, transcending its material envelope by its own powers, sees, feels and hears, in this sublimate etheric substance, all that it desires.

The individual, who very occasionally is permitted a glimpse into this inner world, is presented under two guises to the physical world. Either as a " genius " or a lunatic. In the one case the normal functions of the mind, after its transcendental flight, enable it to express its " impressions " in orderly succession : in the other, mere " babblings " are reproduced, in which the images are distorted and overlaid with the confused " gleanings " in the physical world also. The ultimate " presentations " differ in degree, and arrangement, only.

Eminent psychologists admit how fine is the line which separates genius from insanity. In the case of the genius, it has been inferred that the flights of imagination are occasional only. To this must be added the further limitation that they are rarely made " consciously." That is, the musician, or the painter, does not habitually exercise his will to subdue the normal faculties and open the mind's eye to the " inner light " with a definite purpose. It is more frequently a " casual straying " of the undirected " mind."

Far otherwise is it with the trained clairvoyant. To him, or her, the exercise of the faculty is consciously directed, with set aim, in specific pursuit of knowledge. Although it is generally true that clairvoyants, like painters or poets, are born not made, yet it is essential in each case for the faculty to be trained in its external expression. The child Mozart was " a born musician," but his ripened powers, so far as the transcription of the score was concerned, were the results of bringing his normal functions under control, as well as his " psychic hearing." So with the clairvoyant. The function of inner vision is the natural outcome of the possession of " etheric senses," which one and all possess in embryo.

In the clairvoyant's case it is an instance of a better " balance " between the objective and the subjective worlds, which is constantly being strengthened by use and exercise. To the senses of the mind " matter " is but a shadow, dimly perceived, if at all—the stuff dreams are made of. What to us, with our physical senses, appears as the realm of " reality," is, to the mind, a world of illusion and transitory phenomena, in which "permanence," the only criterion of "reality," is absent. The physical world is essentially one of " change " and not of " permanence." This being so, it will be understood that our three-dimensioned space presents neither difficulty nor obstacle to the inner vision of the clairvoyant. Time in its aspect, to us, of duration, ceases to be. It is merged in the eternal "present."

The astral light may further be considered, in the light somewhat of Haeckel's "substance," as both "force" and "matter." In one aspect it is the material of which the inner vehicle of man is formed, his thought body. It is this etheric, fluidic base, upon which, and into which, the outer, denser, "material" particles of the physical body are built. At death, the mind, wrapped for the time being in its astral envelope, passes out of the physical body on to the next plane. This is practically what happens, in a minor degree, in sleep, more completely in the induced sleep of hypnotism, and more fully still in the "suspended animation" of a protracted trance. At death, however, a final separation is made from the physical envelope. The astral vehicle is sometimes seen by clairvoyants as the phantom of the dead, and occasionally by others, whose hyper-sensitiveness to these visions is usually attributed to the "nerves" being out of order. A diagnosis which is defective. For, far from the nerves being out of order, from the occult standpoint, they have reached a condition of " exaltation " which permits, for the moment, the inhibition of the normal faculties, and allows a transient glimpse, to the partially awakened inner senses, into another world.

In the deepest hypnosis, when the normal senses are absolutely passive, the inner vision of clairvoyance is abundantly manifested. But the more effectual use of the faculty, and in fact the only one which should be " cultivated," is the consciously directed personal exercise. To do this the physical life must be subdued and subordinated to its proper position. A purified and concentrated " will," dominating a positive " thought-output," will inevitably awaken " reflection," the power of the imagination, the eye of the soul or mind, the inner vision. The faculty, in fact, which is the possession, and distinction, of the clairvoyant.

To follow the analogy hinted at previously, the etheric sense of vision which is exercised in clairvoyance may be likened to the power of the X-rays. Just as these rays penetrate matter, which is normally opaque to ordinary light rays, and are obstructed by substances that are transparent to ordinary light rays, so do the etheric senses in clairvoyance transcend the ordinary limitations of space. A light ray will travel from the remotest star and be visible here on earth. No limitation can be placed upon its capacity to travel so long as a medium exists for its transmission. It becomes visible only when there is something to reflect it. But reflected or not, it travels on through infinite space. Thought possesses a similar capacity : but in other directions also. It can travel through space. It can also travel through time. It can search the boundless past, it can rove throughout the infinite present, it can search the limitless future. No fetters can be placed upon thought. It is coextensive with space, and eternal likewise. Not the thought of an individual thinker. But the thought substance, which, in the individual, is a " drop," isolated for purposes of our examination, of the " ocean " of thought.

In this thought ocean, from which we derive our thought substance, the psychoplasm of Haeckel, are stored all the mental experiences, past, present and future. Just as in Mother Earth are stored all the possibilities of form and substance of the physical plane. The blade of grass, the elephant, the man, the hero, the demi-god, all lie physically present in the womb of Mother Earth. The ear of corn, and the man himself, who feeds upon the ear of corn, change places at times. They occupy each the position of the other. The corn becomes the man physically. And the man becomes the corn.

In the eternities, devoid of our illusion of time, the interchange is immediate and present. There is no differentiation. The changes which we perceive taking place in sequence are there seen as an ever-present " Now." This, too, holds good of the etheric realm of thought. Past, present and future may be cognised as the completed and eternal cycle and circle. The present, to us, is merely the shadow of the past, from which it cannot in any way be separated. The future is the extension of the present, with which it is indissolubly bound up.

To this etheric realm, then, the clairvoyant has access. The etheric senses permit the use of the rays which lie beyond the spectrum.

Matter which is opaque to the normal vision is transparent to the eyes of the psychic. The walls of a room, the mountain range, a continent or an ocean, oppose no limitations to the traverse of the etheric sense. Like the light ray, it travels on till it strikes the matter it is in search of, and then illuminates it.

So, when the clairvoyant desires to see events which are happening in distant parts, or to review the past, or to see the future, the grosser senses are laid down and the penetrative rays of the etheric senses brought into action. With the speed of light, space is traversed. Instantaneously, the past or future is surveyed. To effect this transition of consciousness, from one plane of existence to the other, the clairvoyant assumes the trance condition. The normal senses, as in hypnosis, are inhibited. And the mind, freed from its interaction with physical stimuli, reacts to the finer vibrations of the etheric realm. Modern science—psychology—posits the existence of a sub-conscious, or supra-conscious mind. It is this which functions, so it is said, when the normal mind-functions are inhibited. It is this which records, with never-failing accuracy, all that fails normally to impress itself upon the grey substance, to be recovered as ordinary memory.

In hypnosis, of the simpler kinds, it is easy to awaken the memory to records of events that have no power to make themselves available under ordinary conditions. In the deep phases of hypnosis (this is admitted by the text-books of the *exact* sciences), it is possible to induce a condition in which information is obtained from the clairvoyant. The phenomena of clairvoyance is produced by the regular medical practitioner and a disinterested subject. Far-sight, vision at a distance, and penetration of opaque substances, are exhibited under favourable conditions.

In all this, it is urged there is nothing mysterious. There is nothing which is not clearly traceable to the operation of natural laws. The X-ray will penetrate opaque substances and set up chemical dissociations in photographic materials, though such rays are not reflected like ordinary rays, nor do they act as ordinary light rays with regard to our normal vision. It is, therefore, at least possible that in the almost unlimited range of light rays that there are outside our normal vision, there may be, and are, other rays which will react upon the finer, more highly developed senses, the etheric senses, of the clairvoyant.

There can be no real opacity in matter, if matter be, as it is in the last analysis, merely an agglomeration of ether, surcharged with electric force. Eggs will not run through the interstices of an ordinary sieve. But small shot will. Through a sieve with finer apertures flour will pass. And yet we can make a sieve that will hold water. The analogies are rough. But they are intended to shew that our knowledge of the limitations of matter, when we speak of its opacity, is mainly negative. The ordinary attitude is to deny that of which we have no positive knowledge. The telepathist is the Marconi of the occult world. The clairvoyant is merely one step ahead of him.

No one dreams to-day of disputing the fact of wireless telegraphy. There are already a large number of people who are convinced, by practical demonstration, of the truth of telepathy as a normal function for those who are willing to attempt to use it. Before long clairvoyance will have established itself also

8

as a practical possibility for most persons. It will then no longer be an occult art except for those to whom the ordinary functions of everyday science are yet a mystery and an indissoluble marvel.

CHAPTER VII

SPIRITISM

MANY ancient peoples preserved traditions of a race of " divine kings," who ruled over them in a golden age, the more definite recollections of which had long since perished. These great rulers, as befitted their implied superhuman origin, were reputed to have possessed command over natural powers to produce effects mysterious and terrifying. As the remembrance of these divine kings faded a priestly class arose who assumed the divine prerogatives. They claimed no divine origin, but were the accredited guardians of a knowledge which conferred power, amongst others, to raise the "spirits" of the dead, and to hold converse with them. These peoples were distinguished by a high degree of evolution, evidenced by an acquaintanceship with the arts and sciences.

At the opposite pole, in the lowest types of humanity, the same belief in "spiritual forces" may be found. The negro of West Africa, the Malay of Asia, and the Peruvian of America, to say nothing of the Norseman of Europe, all have legends and practices giving support to universal credence in "spiritual forces." The anti-climax is to be found in the adherence of millions to a creed, the essence of which is the belief in the power of "spirit-raising" and "post-mortem communion." This is, of course, Spiritualism. The definition Spiritism, though often confused with Spiritualism (a much narrower issue), really covers a field of far greater scope, and includes all who profess a belief in the survival and energetic manifestation of the "souls" or "spirits" of gods and men.

As it is proposed to deal here with the possibilities of "spirit-raising" from the scientific standpoint, rather than from that of "emotional necessity" for survival, it will be well first to clear the ground. We will agree to call the soul of man the sum of those psychic functions which are correlated to "cerebration." The "spirit" the all-embracing energy of motion: the inherent

116

energy which pervades " substance." Ether, the imponderable, space-filling substance, continuous and non-atomic. Matter, the ponderable, atomic mass whose functions are gravity, inertia, molecular motion or heat, and affinity.

So far we are in total agreement with the definitions of Haeckel. It is when we come to consider the fundamental postulates deduced from those propositions that we differ. " Ether," says Haeckel, " is in eternal motion, and the specific motion of ether, whether we conceive it as vibration, strain, condensation, etc., in reciprocal action with mass movement, gravitation, is the ultimate " cause " of all " phenomena." Matter therefore derives its phenomenal appearance from the movement of ether ; the energy of which or capacity to do work is the inherent power of " spirit " manifestating as " motion."

Since all phenomena owe their objective reality to the movement of ether, it follows that the " cerebration " of the brain is due to the etheric movement we distinguish as "psychic activity," or the functioning of the soul. It is necessary to emphasise this point, as it is sometimes customary to speak of

" force " as a function of " matter." But we cannot conceive of matter (the " product " of the motion of the " ether ") being a " source of motion " if it is at the same time held to be a " consequence " of it.

Psychic activity, then, or soul functioning, is another mode of motion of the ether, one of which is the "materialisation " as objective reality of ordinary " matter." Another " mode " is life, the sum of the determining relative movements associated with the " individuality." The conclusions which we are forced to admit are (1) that matter is merely a transitory form of what, for want of a better name, we term ether ; (2) that ether pervades the whole of space ; (3) that, in essence, that is in its ultimate aspect or condition, it is infinite in extension and eternal in duration ; (4) that ether is ceaselessly in motion ; (5) that this eternal motion we may call spirit.

Further consideration shews us that one of the fundamental laws of objective existence is " periodicity." This is a law whose action calls into being, as an " object " for our material senses, all that is. The operation of this law produces our own phenomenal appearances, as personalities, for the brief

space of an earth-life. The molecular movements of life (and their chemically allied
physiological changes) are due to ether movement, itself the outcome of inherent energy,
spirit. The culmination, so far, of etheric
movement is seen in " psychic activity,"
which dominates the mature personality.

Evolution, due to etheric movement, has
afforded the fittest vehicle for the manifesting of its potencies, for relatively higher
and more complex movements, in the
functioning of the human soul as its present
climax. Ether and its inherent motion are
" eternal," and we cannot therefore admit
the idea that, even when the transitory mode
of its " objective re lity " ceases to manifest,
the etheric motion which caused it ceases to
be. It cannot cease to be, being eternal.

Matter in its essence, as ether, is eternal,
and force or motion is also eternal and inannihilable. Its " mode of manifestation "
may, and does, change. But the sum total,
whether viewed as the " motion " or the
" thing moved," remains constant. Its
cessation of functioning in one form or
mode necessarily implies its re-emergence as
"potential " (passive) or " kinetic " (active)

119

energy in another form or mode. There is no alternative. Persistence of "force" must be postulated for the energy which functions as "psychic activity" as well as for any other mode of motion.

At the moment of physical death such a change of mode occurs. The life motion we regard as "physical," in its relation to chemical and physiological changes in the body itself, changes its mode, from aggregation and association, to segregation and dissociation. The cellular organisation "breaks up." The motion we cognise as "psychic," in relation to its functional activity as the soul, also changes its mode, by withdrawing from the plane of objective reality. It now functions through a less substantial, but still material, vehicle.

All the phenomena of hypnotism substantiate the hypothetical "etheric substratum" body or vehicle. This vehicle is the etheric double, or counterpart, of the physical body, and "persists" for some time as a specific entity after death. It is energised, though faintly only, by the "psychic activity" with which it has been associated during the earth-life of the personality. Its plane of operations is that now spoken of as the " astral," the plane upon which much of our consciousness in " dreams " and " imagination " functions. The power of objective existence, as a materialised personality, has for the moment passed, because the law of " periodicity," which caused its appearance, has now swung back into the period of dissolution.

The persistence of the astral vehicle for a time after death, as a partially conscious entity, which, under certain conditions, may give evidence of its actuality, is the basis upon which rests the entire evidence for spirit appearances, in séances, apparitions of the dead, or dying, and the other phenomena of spirit-raising and demonology. Leaving aside the fact that many of the occurrences reported have been proved to be a mass of trickery, where professional, *i.e.* paid, assistance has been given, there yet remains a considerable volume of " scientifically accredited evidence " which is explicable only on this thesis of the "persistence of psychic activity " after death.

In most cases of "spirit appearances "—in Spiritualism, for example—the presence of a medium is a necessity. His or her " etheric double " is the material used to produce the " simulated appearances." This plastic, imponderable, fluidic substance is energised by the psychic activity of the medium, and assumes a material presentment. This counterfeiting of another form may be accomplished in two ways. Either the disembodied entity is present and assists to make more " material " the partly discarded astral of the medium, or it may be, and usually is, that the " materialisation " is wholly due to those present at the séance. Thought energy is one of the most potent " forces." It functions principally in the ether, and may act in various ways. In telepathy, by etheric vibration and " conscious cerebration "; passively in clairvoyance, as " imagination," by its perception of movements in the astral light. In Spiritism, by the etheric " strain " it imposes, which then compels a plastic, imponderable fluid to assume, for the time, all the qualities of " matter " and any " form " desired.

That the " return of the dead " is accompanied by any good result, either to the disembodied or the circle, is not obvious. The law of evolution demands a constant change of form and mode. The post-mortem state of the dead is, to us, practically one of rest, for the assimilation of its experiences in earth-life. And interruption of this state must necessarily interfere with its further progress. In normal cases " the disembodied entity " is no more able to assist those who still function on the physical plane, than before decease. This is demonstrated by the fact that no knowledge which was not already accessible, has ever been derived from communion with those passed over. This is as might reasonably have been expected. If the disembodied entities of the dead are at rest, they would be making no definite progress in experience or knowledge. It would be impossible, therefore, to obtain from them any further information than that known to them in their earth-life.

But, if it be admitted, as it must be, that there are many stages in human knowledge : that there are those who have progressed far beyond the ordinary boundaries : that there may have been, and be, those who by cultivation of psychic and etheric senses have had access to the infinite records of the akasa or astral realm, then it would follow that there may be some definite gain in communion with these great souls. Now occultism does not sanction commerce with necromancy properly so called. It holds that only evil can result from holding converse with the disembodied entities of normal individuals who have left this earth-life. Such converse, it is said, can give no benefit to the living individual seeking it, and retards the spiritual emancipation of the disembodied soul.

So, on the other hand, converse with those exalted spirits, or great souls, Mahatmas, whose spiritual knowledge and progress have released them from the necessity of further earth-lives, is of benefit to those desiring and seeking it. But this is not necromancy. It is more closely allied to the spiritual communion which is typified by Christian or other religious ecstasy. It is the spiritual dwelling in the "Chrestos" for the uplifting of the material body to its perfection. The words of the great Teacher in the New Testament are pregnant with meaning for those who view the matter with true insight. In the Old Testament we read that the "raising" of the witch of Endor incurred the divine displeasure. But Enoch walked with God.

It may be considered a far cry from the spiritualised emotionalism of religion to the dicta of modern science. Yet there is a link. The older, narrower views of science are widening to a perception of the finer and higher forces which lie behind our world of gross materiality. Philosophy, the unification of the deductions from the laws of scientific phenomena, recedes daily from its mechanistic conception of the universe. The older concepts pressed to their last stronghold are found to be insufficient and unsatisfactory explanations. Forced upon the reason of man is seen the necessity for a re-grouping, or a restatement, of his more fundamental notions.

Philosophy tends to become more spiritualistic and less materialistic. Motion, or the great breath, which stirs from non-manifestation to manifestation, whether we view it as the evolution of a new solar system from homogeneous fire mist, or whether it be the gradual aggregation of the atoms which form the crystal, is sensed as underlying all transitory forms. Motion is the giver and destroyer of form. It is action and reaction. It is life. It is intellect. It is soul. It is spirit. It is the all in all.

This being so, and there being but change, and no annihilation, in the universe, spirit lies back and beyond the material universe of our physical plane. Our personalities are composite. Man, too, is matter and motion, body, soul and spirit. And his soul, his spirit, is capable of responding to, and communion with, his spiritual peers and spiritual superiors, whether disembodied or embodied. Each plane of being, of manifestation, of consciousness, has its laws, its vehicles. With each change, each ascent to a higher sphere, greater possibilities are opened to man. As he evolves, to use the more classic term of modern science, man realises more of his potentialities. The impossible, heretofore, becomes the possible now.

Thus, with the awakening of his latent etheric senses, new worlds are opened for his conquest. By meditation is opened a way for the development of his higher faculties. As the muscle is trained by exercise, so the etheric faculties can be evoked and strengthened. And when the pupil is ready the master is ready to assist him. " Knock and it shall be opened to you " is no spiritual parable. It is a statement of plain speech. For those who desire communion with the great ones, the shining ones, and are willing to prepare themselves, the path is open. But there are many hardships to be undertaken, and to be overcome, before the gateway is passed.

CHAPTER VIII

HYPNOTISM

OUR definition of an occult art will cover hypnotism. For, whilst it is daily practised, more or less consciously, by most of the medical profession, it is yet an unknown art to most others. Moreover, it has been, and in many quarters still is, so discredited that it will bear investigation to sever the fraudulent practices of some of the stage hypnotists from the underlying principles which constitute it a science and an art. The term hypnotism is directly derived from the Greek *hypnos*, "sleep." And here it might be said that as chemistry is the offspring, materialistically, of its parent alchemy, so hypnotism is the daughter of mesmerism. Mesmerism, electrobiology or animal magnetism, were known and practised by the ancients before being rediscovered by Mesmer, the French physician, in the eighteenth century.

It would be difficult to assign a beginning to the practice of the art. In its archaic forms it was probably used coincidently with astrology, spiritism and divination of various kinds, in the most remote past. There is reason to believe that many of the wonders wrought by the most ancient prophets, priests and seers were partly due to the use of hypnotism or animal magnetism. It is possible that they had acquired occult powers and used them freely without deeming it necessary to inquire too closely into the laws of nature which permitted and assisted their operation of these powers. It was sufficient for them that they could accomplish the marvels they desired to exhibit. The earliest recorded instance of what would now be called post hypnotic suggestion was the turning into a pillar of salt of Lot's wife. She had been duly warned. She failed to do as bidden, and the suggestion operated.

Hypnotism, as suggested above, is the materialised form of the older art. It substitutes, for the personal element in sleep induction, the more material forms of physical influence. Whereas in mesmerism the requisite condition of passivity, and

9

amenability to suggestion, was induced in the subject by passes, and the imposition of psychic emanations, in hypnotism this condition is obtained by setting up a stress, physiologically, which reacts upon the psychic mechanism. This is done in various ways. Essentially the condition is procured by concentration of the attention by means of the sense of vision or of hearing. A bright light on which the eyes are steadfastly fixed, or a sound constantly repeated, on which attention is concentrated, such as the ticking of a watch, will inevitably, in the absence of other physical stimuli, set up a strain which results in fatigue and sleep. This, in simple terms, is hypnosis. Nothing more, nor less, than an artificially procured strain which leaves the subject in a condition physically resembling that of sleep, but with the motor mechanism hyper-sensitive to stimulation by the operator.

Now it is necessary to remember that in the normal waking state the actions are controlled by the will. The will itself is exercised as the result of reflection on the train of ideas passing through the mind. The ideas passing through the mind are produced primarily by the perception of sensations affecting the senses. I see a man striking a child. The sense of vision permits and induces in my mind the mental picture. My understanding and my memory, by association of ideas, enable me rapidly to reflect upon this. My judgment is that this is wrong and must be stopped. My will determines my action. I rush off to the place and exert myself to stop the ill-treatment of the child. Or it may be that my ears have been assailed by the cries of the child, though I was unable actually to see what was occurring. In any case, the result would probably be the same. I should try to locate the sound and stop the cruelty. It is evident, then, here, that the starting point of the train of actions is the sense impression. If my ears as well as my eyes had been insensible to that sensation, the train of ideation, understanding, emotion and volition would not have happened.

If it be possible now to substitute, for the normal sensations and perceptions, a wholly artificial train, the result will be the same, for all practical purposes, upon the mechanism of the body of the subject. The normal functioning of the senses is inhibited by the production of the artificial sleep condition—hypnosis,—but a relationship is preserved between the operator and the subject. The subject sees with the operator's eyes, hears with his voice, and is affected psychically by his mental processes. This in short is suggestibility. In the normal waking state this suggestibility is seen in operation. Most of all our so-called exact knowledge or science is accepted upon faith. We trust the teller. We accept blindly the assertion of the scientist. In a dynamo room, if we are told that to touch a bare wire from the pole of the alternator would cause death as by a lightning stroke, we accept it and act upon it. We refrain from touching. This massive, tangible globe we inhabit, we believe to be a tiny atom whirling on its own axis, and at an inconceivable pace through space, and that it has been doing so for countless æons. And so with other dicta of astronomy and the other sciences. We act upon the suggestions made by others believing that they will work. And they do.

The actor, the preacher, the lawyer, the orator, the painter, the sculptor, all make use of this susceptibility to suggestion of the normal waking state. And in so far as we are satisfied with the intrinsic value of their art, we permit ourselves to be influenced by their suggestions. The least educated of us are perhaps more susceptible to suggestion in the waking state. This is merely to assert that the plastic material of the brain substance is amenable to less and less suggestion as it becomes used more. This is just what might be expected. In early childhood the susceptibility to suggestion is greatest. The material is a blank sheeting waiting for the designs to be etched in. Moment by moment impressions are received and stored. Fresh sensations supervene. The earlier ones are modified and amplified, and in some instances eradicated, and the newer ones substituted.

Education, or the acquisition of knowledge, is the extension of the stored impressions of sensations. It is the ordered sequence and association for purposes of comparison and contrast of the perceptions. This knowledge is either direct (that is derived from actual sensations, sensory impressions), or indirect (that is attained by suggestion). The difference is a real one. But the actual value for purposes of understanding and will is much the same. Comparatively speaking, very few people have toured around the world. Yet most of us have very definite impressions, received suggestively, by oral teaching, by reading, by pictures, or by photographs, of the sensations actually recorded by those more fortunately circumstanced. So long as we are credulous, so long do we receive and act upon suggestions thus received. To us they are real : using the term somewhat loosely.

In hypnosis, the relation between operator and subject is almost similar to that of teacher and pupil. The primary condition is practically one of trust. There is, then, an acceptance of suggestion as of reality. The suggestion is accepted and acted upon as if it were in truth sensation, perception and ideation. The antecedent condition to the development of the hypnosis is the credulous stage. To use a photographic simile the brain is sensitised by expectancy and awaits the exposure to suggestion. The latent image then proceeds, automatically, to develop.

This stage of credulity is the link which enables the transfer of volition from subject to operator. Before hypnosis begins the subject surrenders himself more or less

134

wholly to the suggestions of the operator. The artificial sleeping condition is procured by the physical stress primarily and directly, but it is preceded mentally by the idea that the operator will induce this condition and control the actions later of the subject. As the subject passes into the elementary hypnotic stage it is with this idea predominant in his mind. His own purposiveness has vanished. He becomes a machine animated by the artificial sensations, of suggestion, given by the operator. It is well that this should be made quite clear, because upon this link depends the power of control.

Suggestion, normally, in the waking state is visional or verbal. That is, the ideas set in train result from what we read or see or hear. In the elementary stages of hypnosis the suggestions are also verbal or visional. But with the passing of the subject into the deeper stages mental suggestion is sufficient. Automatism resulting from imitation is a well-marked phase in early hypnosis. The operator, having secured the attention of his subject, and made him amenable to suggestion in the manner indicated, will himself begin a series of motions he desires imitated. The subject responds immediately by copying the motion, and then continues it automatically until commanded to stop. Similarly, having been induced to sleep, or even before that condition is reached, if the subject be suggestively told that he cannot move, or cannot speak, hear nor see, taste nor smell, his activities will be limited in each of these directions. His normal sense perceptions are inhibited at the will of the operator.

On the other hand, it is equally possible to make him see, hear, smell, taste or touch things not actually present, but suggested to him as being so. If the subject be told that his tooth is aching it aches. If he be told that a mad dog is present he will see the dog and try to evade it. If told to eat a piece of raw potato which it is suggested is an apple or a peach, all the customary taste sensations will be experienced. If given an imaginary baby to nurse he will hold it and feel its weight, though nothing tangible is there.

Suggestion is followed by sensation. Suggestion to him is tantamount to sensation. If touched on the face with a damp cloth and told it is a hot iron he will experience the sensation of burning. If the suggestion be

136

carried yet further, the flesh itself can be made to respond to the suggestion and a wound actually be produced. If told to commit an action the command is unhesitatingly obeyed. If restricted in action by an imaginary condition that also is obeyed. A chalk-mark on the floor, or even a pretended chalk-mark, accompanied by a suggestion that it is an impassable barrier, will prove so to the subject. He sees the barrier that the operator mentally projects and verbally insists upon.

Suggestion may be for immediate action, or for deferred action. If the latter, the suggestion will be acted upon at the time commanded although a long period of normal action may supervene. This is post suggestion. A subject told to stab a person with an imaginary dagger handed to him by the operator may shew hesitation or even disinclination at first. But repeated hypnoses will lessen the resistance. The subject becomes more and more amenable to suggestion, until neither hesitation nor resistance is shewn to any command imposed upon him.

In hypnosis there are several well-defined states. The earliest, the credulous, is almost

137

a waking state, in which the control of the operator inhibits the ordinary senses and substitutes his suggestions for sensations. The sleeping state, which easily follows it, by suggestion, is cataleptic. A deeper phase is the lethargic, and this in turn is followed by the somnambulic and lucid stages. Lethargy, or heavy slumber, from which it seems almost impossible to waken the sleeper, by ordinary means, is a fairly well-known condition. The first sleep in hypnosis is inclined to be lethargic, but quickly passes by suggestion into the cataleptic phase. In this condition rigidity of the limbs, with eyes opened, and the functions of the heart and lungs reduced to a minimum, is observed.

Pronounced catalepsy can hardly be discriminated from death. There is complete fixation of the limbs. The pulse becomes almost unobservable, and the circulation of the blood declines. There is perfect insensibility to pain. An eyeball may be stroked without a flicker. A needle may be passed through the flesh without shrinking on the part of the subject. The action of the pulse or the heart-beat may be quickened or reduced. Blood will flow or not from an incision into

138

the flesh, as suggested. The catalepsy may be prolonged almost indefinitely or discontinued easily by suggestion and passes.

In the cataleptic condition the fixation of the limbs and the trunk is such that the body of the subject will support, without trouble, the weight of several individuals, whilst it is itself suspended by head and heels only from these two points. It has all the appearance of *rigor mortis.* Nervous and muscular activity have wholly vanished. If pushed from the erect position the body falls like a log of wood overturned from the vertical. By suggestion and passes the limbs may be placed in any position of extension or flexion, and will so remain until released. The subject is unable to move a muscle. He has first to be mentally and verbally restored to the more normal condition, or his limbs physically moved by the operator.

The cataleptic condition is easily induced from the first light lethargy which ensues in early hypnosis by suggesting inflexibility to the subject. An arm is extended. He is told he cannot bend it, and he cannot. Passes are made, and it is suggested that his body is becoming stiff. It is becoming more

139

and more rigid. And as the suggestions are given the body responds by assuming a condition of rigid inflexibility. The anæsthetic effect in catalepsy is perfect. Surgical operations may be performed even more successfully than under a normal anæsthetic such as chloroform or ether.

But it is the higher degrees of hypnosis with which we are more concerned as an occult art—the somnambulic and lucid phases. In these the subject betrays distinct powers of psychometry, clairaudience and clairvoyance. With the eyes closed, a book or a sealed letter will be read. Conversations taking place in a distant part of the house will be heard and may be reproduced. Visions of what is transpiring long distances away will be more or less accurately described. The subject becomes possessed for the time being of the powers of the trained psychic.

It requires, however, the volition of the operator to evoke these powers. And it is at his command only that they are exercised and the results of such exercises made available. The subject, when awakened, is quite unconscious of the experiences, and will not credit that he has made such assertions as he

140

has done when in the hypnotic state. And only in the hypnotic condition can the memory of past activities in a similar state be recovered. In the intervals of normal life between hypnoses all recollection is lost.

Physical contact with an object will permit the subject to reproduce the circumstances under which it was used and, psychometrically, to reconstruct the scenes in which it took a part. The differences should be noted here, between the states of lucidity and suggestibility. In the latter the subject would be guided entirely by the suggestions of the operator. The object would then appear to him in whatever form the latter desired. In the lucid stage the subject shews true psychometric power.

Instances might be multiplied of the faculties exhibited by the hypnotised subject in the lucid phases. But little purpose would be served by this. There is a considerable literature on the subject which those who desire may consult. Scores, nay hundreds and thousands, of thoroughly authenticated experiments are recorded. The phenomena of magnetism may be referred to briefly here. Ordinary magnets are used. These, presented by a single pole, to a polar zone of the body, may be used to induce certain of the hypnotic phases.

By reversing the poles a change of state physically and mentally will result. A suggestion given to perform an action may be modified, alternated or even reversed by changing the polarity of the magnetic currents which are discernible in the body during hypnosis. These currents are amenable to the passes made by the operator, with the hands, and it is by means of them that the nerve centres are controlled in catalepsy, or that all muscular activity may be discontinued in the subject. For healing purposes, too, the currents are used.

Ill health, ultimately, is a question of lowered or accelerated vibration rate of the etheric particles of the body. When the cause is mental, primarily, as in nervous breakdown, it reacts upon the physical. When alternatively it is physical, primarily, the sensations affect the mental activities. Whether it be a cancerous growth, or toothache, essentially it is the same. The tissues are disordered and the mental activities are deranged. There is always action and reaction between the two.

142

Restore tone to the tissues, and the mental activities respond. Harmonise or produce an orderly sequence in the mental activities, and the physical body responds.

The physical particles of the body, in ultimate analysis, are but force centres and ether whirls. Their grosser aggregations are but transitory forms changing, imperceptibly perhaps, but still changing, moment by moment. When the aggregations are deranged, the magnetic currents which circulate are out of synchronism. The mechanism is out of gear with itself. It is "jumping" instead of running smoothly. The imposition of a strong current will reduce the disorder. It will restore the polarity of the whole. It will cause the mechanism to resume its orderly swing. The power of curing was illustrated by the belief in the efficacy of the laying on of hands. In this was seen the dynamic effect of a personal current of magnetism which would suffice to heal the sick and calm those mentally afflicted and distressed.

Now, wonderful as are the instances given of the powers exhibited in hypnosis, there is in them nothing to conflict with the dicta of material science. All action is the result of stimuli. And whether we consider this as the tropistic movement of the convoluta—a little plant animal—or the most admirable aspirations of a noble man, in his attempts to realise his highest ideals, we see the resulting action as the necessary reaction to the stimulus. There is no freedom. All that we do, think, plan, reflect, scheme, design or suggest is the outcome and effect of stimulus from without. In hypnosis it is the same. The elementary stimuli are such as to produce an apparent torpor of the motor units and system. Thereafter, the link having been established, the process of stimulation and action goes on, the operator being merely the channel or vehicle through which, and by which, the stimuli enter and control the subject. This, of course, so far as the earlier phases are concerned.

In the deeper stages there is a liberation of the psychic or etheric senses, because the normal senses are inhibited. The subconscious self is permitted freedom of action and reaction because the limitations of the normal activities have been overcome. There is in this no disturbance of natural law. It is only an extension of it. The perceptions are

144

heightened, because the consciousness now functions on a higher plane. The stimuli to which it responds are more subtle. The vibrations are etheric rather than material.

Religious ecstasy—the illumination of the converted—is due to this relief of limitation. There is an escape of the consciousness to the higher planes of being. There is a sympathetic outreach to the oversoul. Fresh points of view are taken. The whole perspective is changed. The mode of life is altered. Fresh standards are imposed on the lower nature. The guidance is accepted of the higher principles, and there is a consciousness of the receipt of grace. The Christ within, the God overhead, have become manifest.

And because of this, hypnotism becomes either a great power for good or for evil. It may be used in this way to evoke the divine principles within, to enlighten the life, and to guide it aright, or it may be used by the evolution of these same powers, of extended vision and capacity, to do evil, because the operator may use them for his own selfish and evil ends. And as mankind is yet more prone to evil than to good, it is desirable that a positive action of mind should be cultivated.

10   145

An appeal, then, should be addressed to the powers within to guide and direct aright the use of these extended faculties which in due time will be habitually used as man moves forward to the conquest of his greater kingdom.

CHAPTER IX

GEOMANCY

NOT one of the least difficult to defend of the occult arts is the practice of astrological geomancy. That it should be possible to forecast events, to prophesy in short, by a consideration of marks made on the earth, or on a piece of paper, by an individual who must be careful to abstain from consciously directing his actions, seems in the highest degree to be absurd. The position is stated accurately. It is not overdrawn. For the practice of geomancy requires merely, as an essential, an indefinite number of points to be made by an inquirer who shall not consciously decide what that number shall be.

That these dots, or punctuation marks, should be made at set times is a desideratum, but not an essential. The process of divination briefly is this. A wand or stick, if the earth is to be used, or a pencil or pen, if paper be used, is held in the right hand. The matter to be elucidated is then framed as a question. Concentrating his mind on the question to which an answer is sought, a number of points is made on the material used, in four successive lines. Each line is then pointed off from the right in " twos." If the result is an even number of dots or points in the first line, two is taken thus, . . , as the head of the first figure. The second line, which gives the neck, is similarly treated. If this gives an odd number of points, one is placed thus, . , immediately under the two. The figure now assumes this form ˙ . ˙ The third line is treated in the same manner, and gives the body, thus, if even, . . The figure is then ˙ . ˙ The fourth line, which gives the feet, is added to the others, and, if odd, completes the first figure thus, ˙ . ˙

In succession three more figures are created, from further lines of points or dots. These are the four mothers. From them are formed the four daughters. This is done by taking all the " heads " of the mothers, which are
148

placed one beneath the other to form the first daughter. The "necks," "bodies" and "feet," similarly treated, give the other three figures. From the eight geomantic figures thus produced, the mothers and daughters, the four nephews are formed. This is done by adding the points of the heads of the first two figures together, and if odd marking one, if even two. The necks, bodies and feet added together give the other points for the first nephew.

Figures three and four give the second nephew, and so on. From the four nephews are now constructed two witnesses, and from the two witnesses the judge. Each of the latter three figures is constructed in a similar method to that for producing the nephews themselves. It will be seen that it is the first set of lines of marks or dots which govern the whole of the subsequently produced figures. And it is specially impressed upon the inquirer that he should ponder carefully upon his question to the exclusion of all other thoughts whilst pointing off. The idea underlying the instruction being, of course, that a superior agency to the normal mind will influence the hand in making the required marks.

For the interpretation of the figures, geo-mancy depends upon astrology. To each of the fifteen figures which are practically made as above, a significance, astrologically, is appended. For a very simple determination of the question the two witnesses and the judge are used. Further elucidation is given by consulting in addition the replies which are furnished by the other figures.

To obtain a complete answer a perfect astrological figure is constructed. Into this are inserted, in a given order, the various geomantic figures, and the reading is modified by the bearing which the other figures assume mutually in agreement or otherwise. The significances of the geomantic figures have doubtless been empirically discovered and codified by hosts of experimenters, who have handed down to their disciples the results of their experiences. The seeker for occult knowledge is advised himself to follow the same example. He should keep a book in which his experiments are recorded, so that he may see how accurately his prophecies may actually occur. He is advised, however, to conduct such experiments in a reverent and devout attitude, and not to attempt divination till he has mastered the principles upon which the art depends. Nor should attempts be made in a spirit of idle curiosity. Only by a thorough understanding of the underlying laws is dependable information to be had.

No man would expect to become an artist because he had been handed a case of colours and some brushes. He must first study the elements of drawing and the art of colours. He has, in fact, to acquire the technique of the art. And then only by the exercise of his creative imagination can he hope to become an artist. So with the geomantist. He must first study the principles of the art. A knowledge of astrology must be obtained. And this is no simple matter. It requires immense application to acquire the elements of the science, so stupendous are its ramifications. To apply them to the solution of geomantic problems requires also the interpretative capacity born only of long study and meditation.

It will not be possible here to do more than indicate very roughly the principal lines of the science. This work is concerned more with the presentation of conclusions that the occult arts are based upon real facts in nature.

Those who desire practical help in the arts themselves are referred to the vast literature on the subject, particulars of some of which will be appended to this volume. There are two great divisions of astrological influence, the zodiacal and the planetary. These modify and augment each other.

To deal with the planetary influences first, it will be necessary to clear the ground of a popular misconception. This is that astrology is associated only with the physical influences of the planets. In the chapter dealing with astrology itself, it is pointed out that it is difficult, if not impossible, to draw the line between the physical and the psychic. It is now proposed to carry that argument a step further. Though the astrologer calculates from the appearances and positions of the celestial bodies he is not bound solely by their physical aspect.

The sun, for example, astrologically, is not merely the blazing photosphere, chromosphere and nucleus we observe in the heavens in the daytime, and which scientifically we know to be the source of all our physical energies here. It connotes to the astrologer, in his spiritual science, the supreme lord, the source of

152

wisdom, of love and of intelligence. The physical sun is but the vestment and the vehicle of that vast fount of life and love and intelligence which is manifested in man, as he, too, functions on the various planes of his being. For man is the universe in miniature. He is the microcosmos. In him are embodied all the powers of the universe, did he but know it. And by virtue of this he is in correspondence with, animated and energised by, the great powers which have their physical emblems in the planets as the seat of their grosser activities.

Each of the planets, then, typifies an outflow of power, and these, acting in unison, or in opposition, affect individual man as may be determined. Philosophically this may be seen to be quite true. The universe, man included, is ultimately mass and motion, and if will be taken to represent motion, and ideation mass, we may easily credit the influences which are said to affect man's course in life, to the great planetary and other celestial powers.

Zodiacal powers are ascribed to the great celestial belt through which the earth appears to travel in its path around the sun. The belt

153

is divided into twelve signs, or houses, and each of these is said to exercise a sharply defined influence on those born in its sphere of dominion. Astrological works give detailed references to the general characteristics of those born under the various signs. Disposition and temperament, mental and physical activities and deficiencies are indicated, and undoubtedly these general indications are, broadly speaking, true in the main. They shew in a marked degree the tendencies which appear most prominent in the various classes of individuals. They do certainly shew capacities and abilities which in many cases may not mature, though most decisively they are actually present.

It is here, naturally, that the astrologer sees the action of the planetary influences which modify considerably the more general tendencies of the zodiacal ruling. The permutations are almost uncountable. So too are the diversities of human nature. Many individuals approximate very closely to type. But all have differences which are characteristic. The conjunctions and oppositions of the planetary and zodiacal influences are held to account for these.

154

When it is remembered how simple in essence man is, how insignificant the causes which determine, in the first place, any particular train of thought and action, it will be granted that his elementary motions are, perhaps, largely determined by influences of which normally he is not cognisant. Physically we know he is always obsessed by meteorological conditions. Even such radical functions as his growth and reproduction are determined by physical stimuli.

Geomantic problems should be propounded at suitable times. The days of the week are named by their ruling planets. Each planet rules the first hour of his day. The planets follow in a definite order. Any day chosen is divided, from sunrise to sunset, adding an hour for twilight, into twelve equal parts. The first period, or twelfth part, is ruled by the planet of the day, and the others follow in proper order. Saturn, for example, typifies the earth, and therefore rules agriculture and mining. A problem affecting either of these pursuits should, preferentially, be proposed at a time when the planetary body concerned is in the ascendant. The reason for this should be obvious. At such a time the influences of the planet—the psychical influence as well as the physical—might more certainly be depended upon to guide the inquirer.

To construct the perfect astrological figure, the reader is advised to consult *Geomancy* by Franz Hartmann (Rider, 3s. 6d. net). A few particulars may be given here just to shew briefly the principles involved. The complete figure is divided into twelve houses. Each of these is dominated by a planet or planets, whose influence must be studied in reference to the others. The various houses are allocated to the several phases or vicissitudes of life. Thus house VIII. deals particularly with death, legacies, trouble, suffering and poverty, whilst house XI. deals with protection, riches, presents, friends, joy, hope, confidence. To the planetary signs are added the zodiacal signs, to obtain the full indications of the influences in the problem.

Rules are given in the text-books for the insertion in the astrological house of the first figure geomantically obtained. The others then follow in definite sequence. As was said, each of the geomantic figures is allied to certain planets. The planetary influences are inter-related to those of the zodiac. The first mother is put into house I., and the zodiacal sign related to her is put next and adjoining it. The others follow in numerical order, though an alternative method is given for placing the figures. In the latter case, as the ruling would be different, an alternative method of allocating the position of the judge is also given. This, in effect, produces a similar result to that previously obtained by the other arrangement. The specific claim made for geomancy is that it provides a means for the stimulation of the spiritual faculties. In its essence the science is alchemical. It is concerned with the transmutation of the celestial correspondences into spiritual truth and light, and the life of fleshly observation into the eternal outgrowth of spiritual existence.

By teaching man to observe the motions of the heavenly bodies it teaches him also to learn to analyse his own being. In him, as in the planets, resides the animus mundi, the spirit of creation. In him is hidden, waiting to be evoked, the spirit of truth. For man is mineral, plant, animal and god. But he has to be awakened before he can exercise his higher powers of spiritual intuition. The methods of geomancy provide merely the vehicle of manifestation for the spiritual outpouring. A gross body, so to speak, for the divine elements in man to exhibit their powers. And only as man learns to use these powers wisely, unselfishly, and in harmony with the divine law and order of the universe, will their full secrets be opened to him. Whilst he dares to strive to wrest them for idle and selfish ends, he will be frustrated of his main object. He may achieve some little mastery of them, but they will be illusory, and often work to his own undoing.

In an earlier chapter we believe the truth has been demonstrated of the proposition that astrology may claim to rank as an exact science. It remains to find the connecting link between the astrological data used and the apparently haphazard, and unconscious, use of them for geomantic prophecy. Unconsciousness gives the key to the problem. The essential condition, it was urged, was that the inquirer should not direct the number of the marks. In this way it was to be obvious that the figures produced should not be chosen consciously. The normal powers of reason were to be inhibited.

Apparently chance was to be allowed its opportunity. But there is no such thing as chance. Every movement, even if unconsciously made, is determined. "Not a sparrow falls to the ground" without a determining cause. The formation of the figures, then, had a cause. We have to ascertain, now, what that cause was; and if it be proved that a definite celestial influence may be assigned to the chance markings, it will be held that the art of geomancy has been triumphantly vindicated. The key is not difficult to seek.

From the purely materialistic standpoint man is held to possess a subconscious mind. It is this portion of the mind which acts in times of sheer physical stress or exhaustion. It is this portion of the mind which is closely inter-related with the oversoul. It is the subconscious self, or the subliminal consciousness, which never sleeps. It is this which is the crude organ by which premonitions and prevision are received. It is this which holds the mental records of all experiences. It is this which functions so largely in natural somnambulists and in hypnotic mediums.

Normally, as has been seen, the subliminal

159

consciousness is inhibited. The ordinary waking consciousness clouds it and clogs its action. But it is ceaselessly active on its own plane. It is only that it is not allowed to make itself heard. This subliminal consciousness is the germ of the etheric senses—the senses which when awakened have access to the divine records. The records which, in their eternal essence, embody past, present and future in an omnipresent now. By virtue of their capacity these ethereal senses are intimately related to the great spiritual powers of the universe ; the powers which manifest their activity on the physical plane through the vestments of the planets. But their spiritual essences are not confined to the locality in which their physical bodies reside. As a man's thoughts leave him and radiate in all directions, impinging upon, and reacting through, and with, other thoughts and on other minds, so do these great influences stir the whole cosmos of ideation.

What is thought ? What is ideation ? Does man secrete thought as he does bile ? Are his ideas the product of metabolism ? We trow not. The thoughts of man are his inbreathings of the celestial oversoul. His

160

ideas shape themselves from the inflow of the spiritual essence of ideation which causes the universe to be. Man is as his thoughts make him. Man is no greater than his ideas. And both are due to influences outside him. And if, as in the case of the sun, we may cognise a direct physical sequence of energy and movement and reaction, so in the spiritual sun we may see the source of the higher powers.

When we consider, therefore, the directions for self study and self analysis ; when we realise that a man has to train his spiritual nature to respond to these higher impulses ; when we think of the time and effort involved in awakening these higher centres and in teaching the consciousness to carry over the results of its researches, then we may see that the practice of geomantic astrology is no thing to be lightly undertaken. Nor can its helpful inspirations be grasped by the thoughtless and merely curious. It is *divination*: commune with the Divine. And only to those who attune themselves to the rarity of its vibrations, with pure and unselfish motives, is given the full measure of its greatness.

11

To others, who for selfish or ignoble ends pursue it, a measure of success may be accorded, but this is both illusive and dangerous. It is dabbling in the black arts and is allied to sorcery and necromancy. It is abuse of the divine spark. It is an inversion of godly power. And those who thus misuse their divine inheritance will fall into the outer darkness. These occult powers and possibilities are available for all. No hindrance is placed upon their cultivation and use beyond the efforts necessary to develop them. And it is in this that perhaps lies the best proof of their validity. They work. Those who will conscientiously study on the lines laid down may, by personal experience, prove for themselves the facts which are advanced by others to whom proofs, in due time, have likewise been accorded.

CHAPTER X

PALMISTRY

ONE of the least reputable, but most constantly practised of the occult arts, is palmistry. It would be difficult to find any individual of mature age, perhaps, who has not at some time had his or her palm read. Generally there is a good-humoured contempt for the reader and for the reading, but, nevertheless, the most sceptical have given way to the blandishments of the cheiromantist. The fashionable professors of the art, who practise in Bond Street and have their scale of charges in guineas, are as frequently consulted as the more modest Gypsy, who invades the country cottage, or wanders down the area steps, ostensibly to sell the products of their handicraft, but more often to beguile the maids with the prospects of good fortune indicated in their hands. And if it is more usually the fair sex, with their attributed fatal curiosity, who are the more eager for a reading, the sterner sex, too, must not be exempted from falling a victim to the claims of the art.

Life's disappointments are many. But hope springs eternal in the human breast. Anything, therefore, which will afford some ground for justifying the hope of better things is generally seized with avidity. Besides which the imagination, that superb faculty of the human mind, itself forecasts the future, but mistrusting its own powers to ensure their materialisation, desires always some corroboration. And this corroboration, of the dreams of a brighter future, palmistry often affords.

Like most of the other occult arts, palmistry or cheiromancy had its rise in the dim past. It is known to have been practised in very early ages by the Brahmins of India. References may be found in the Old Testament which suggest that it was known as a secret art by the children of Israel, who had perhaps borrowed the practice, as they did other secret and forbidden arts, from their neighbouring nations. Cheiromancy was well known to Aristotle. This great Grecian philosopher

164

discovered a valuable treatise on the subject, a gold-lettered volume, which he presented to Alexander the Great. The work was afterwards translated into Latin by Hispanus, and became a classic. The Roman emperors, too, were not unaddicted to the practice of palmistry, if contemporary history is to be credited. The annals of the middle ages record several well-known exponents of the art who have left contributions to the literature of the subject. Hartlieb, who wrote *Die Kunst Ciromantia*, 1448, and Cocles, *circa* 1504, the latter of whom predicted accurately his own murder, are outstanding examples. Later there was Marie Anne Lenormand, 1772–1843, who foretold the downfall of Napoleon Bonaparte, as recorded in *Souvenirs Prophetiques d'une Sibylle.*

Of the history of palmistry little more need be said. It has been closely associated with the Gypsies, who claim to be of oriental and ancient descent. Sometimes, indeed, they assert their descent from the Egyptians who were scattered from their native land because they failed to pay tribute to the Virgin and her Divine Son. At other times they maintain that they possess, in unbroken heritage, the lore of their Chaldean forefathers.   Possibly neither hypothesis is strictly accurate.

Borrow, whose researches in Gypsy language were so extensive and continuous as to constitute him in that particular field a philologist of no mean order, appears to prove, linguistically, the direct descent of the Rommany tongue from Sanskrit and Persiac.   There is no doubt, also, that for some thousands of years the Gypsies, like the Jews, have been a race apart.   They have retained their own customs and habits, and, while borrowing from, and adapting themselves to, the countries in which they have made their temporary homes, they have neither intermarried with the natives, nor lost their vagrant and uncivilised mode of living.

They are nature's vagabonds.   They live close to their mother, and it may be because of this that they are able to read the signs which nature offers more easily than others. Living by his wits, at the expense of the least possible physical effort, the Gypsy is usually a skilled physiognomist, a shrewd psychologist and—a rare rogue.   That he possesses, in addition, undoubted occult powers of a low order, is a matter of general belief, which has been justified by the fulfilment of his predictions on many occasions.

Palmistry, as a science and an art, falls under three aspects, viz., cheirognomy, cheirosophy, and cheiromancy. The first is the art of recognising the tendencies of intelligence as suggested by the form of the hands; the second, the scientific study of the comparative values of hand formations; and the third, the art of divination from the lines and markings of the hands, and the form of hand and fingers. As popularly practised, palmistry depends upon a knowledge of the first two plus other qualities which will be referred to later. In the ordinary delineations of the professional palmist, little account, so far as the client is concerned, is paid to anything else but the divination of the future.

But it must be remembered that the deductions on which the prognostications are based are made from the knowledge of the former science applied to the hand under survey. A palmist would therefore study first the shape and general characteristics of the hand as a whole, then proceed, by analysis, to a consideration of the parts and details, and finally to a separate appreciation of the various

167

lines and markings. Such information as would be derived from this procedure would be synthesised for the client. Broad tendencies and disposition would be ascertained from cheirognomy, and by cheirosophy, and from the reading of the hand itself would be constructed the course of the future.

Hands are divided into types, and general characteristics are associated with each type. Six or seven of these " types " are the usual divisions. One classification, for example, gives the elementary, large - palmed hand ; the necessary, with spatulated or spade-shaped fingers ; the artistic, with conical-shaped fingers ; the useful, with square - shaped fingers ; the knotted, or philosophical ; the psychic, pointed ; and the mixed, in which the types are blended with none in particular predominant.

Another classification gives the following :— Short hands, impulsive judgment without analysis ; long hands, capacity for detail ; hard, firm hands, energy and perseverance ; soft, loose hands, laziness ; smooth hands, impressionality, inspiration, intuition ; knotted hands, reflection, order, science. These, from independent authorities, shew great similarities. This might have been expected, since cheirognomy may be ranked as an exact science. Modern research, in its tabulation and comparison of observation, has shewn that such classifications are justifiable and accurate. From a comprehensive survey, of a large number of cases, it has been demonstrated that hands of various types are associated with individuals who also conform generally to the type or class in which they would be placed otherwise by reason of such correspondences in the shape of the hands.

Next in order to the shape of the hands, comes the consideration of the form of the fingers. These details, as suggested above, are both general and particular in their determination. General inasmuch as the form as a whole, whether pointed, square-shaped, spatulate or otherwise, give generic tendencies; particular because each digit is assigned a special sphere of influence. The thumb, for example, is one of the principal significators—to use an astrological term. It represents the man, born of love and life. Its size determines whether reason and intellect, or sentiment and emotion, will be predominant in his nature. The first phalange indicates the comparative intensity of will, the second of reason, and the third of love.

It is not sufficient to read from one hand only. Both must be compared, since the activity of the right may reasonably be expected to modify the passivity of the left. The first finger is the finger of Jupiter, the second of Saturn, the third of Apollo, and the fourth of Mercury. The disposition of the fingers, when the hand is held open, gives general indications which modify, verify, or amplify the indications drawn from the other sources. At the bases of the fingers lie the mounts of Jupiter, Saturn, Apollo, and Mercury. At the base of the thumb lies the mount of Venus; opposing it is the mount of Luna. Their extent, magnitude, or absence, give corresponding qualities. Virtues pushed to excess become vices. Religious feeling and commendable ambitions run riot may easily develop into pride or arrogant intolerance and tyranny : their negation may be expressed by irreligion and vulgarity.

For purposes of divination, or foretelling the future, the lines of the hand are consulted. The principal of these are the lines of life, head, heart, fate, and fortune. Around the

170

wrist should be found the triple bracelet, shewing the lines of health, wealth, and happiness. The line of life runs from just below the centre of the palm, around the base of the thumb, almost to the wrist. The line of head starts from the same point as the line of life, and in some cases, for part of its length, runs coincident with it. Usually it crosses the palm, descending towards the wrist as it traverses the hand. The line of heart runs partly across the palm above the head line. The line of fate intersects the two latter lines, nearly at right angles ; starting well above the centre of the palm, it runs towards the wrist, from which it assumes the vertical position. The line of fortune, which rises in the mount of Apollo, runs down towards the wrist, parallel to the line of fate.

Generally, a deep, firm line, of narrow width has good significance, with the single exception of the line of health, which, if presented too prominently, denotes a weakened constitution. The line of intuition is not generally found except in those possessing a fair share of this faculty. The extent of the lines and their freedom from interruptions connote the continuity or otherwise of their

171

signification. The coincidences of lines and their parallelisms also modify their normal indications. It is not proposed to give here detailed particulars of the lines and other data which, aggregated, afford the delineation of character and life cycle. There are plenty of books on the subject which may be consulted. Our concern is only to shew that evidence may be abundantly produced to justify a belief in the truth and value of palmistry as an art.

As with the other occult arts, the validity of palmistry depends upon the care with which its principles have been constructed and formulated. Phrenology and physiognomy to-day do not require apologetics. But it is not so long ago that it would have been necessary to defend them by the same line of argument as will be pursued here for the others. Anatomical knowledge of the brain structure, enriched by biological research, and interpreted by the dicta of experimental psychology, has assigned different regions of the brain structure to the various phases of cerebration. An injury to one portion of the brain has resulted in the inhibition of a certain faculty.

Further than this, it has been demonstrated that certain forms of cranial structure, and obviously of brain material, have been found to be present in individuals of strongly marked type. When those indications, physiologically, were missing, corresponding deficiencies were observed, mentally. There was a coincidence to be noted between the physical organ and its psychical inhabitant. Thus grew up the exact science of phrenology. So, too, with physiognomy. The form and comparative sizes of the facial organs were found to correspond with marked types of mental development on certain lines.

Cheirognomy and cheirosophy have arisen in the same way. Correspondences were noted between those with outstanding traits of character and the physical conformation of the hands. From broad generalisation these became more and more exact, until the areas of correspondence were accurately located and finely analysed. A constant appeal was made from theory to fact, and thus the evidence of probability was strengthened till it was accounted dependable and scientific.

Now, granting that distinctions may be made between the mind and the body—that

173

differences may be perceived and commented on between the instrument and the musician, —is not this what might have been expected ? Taking even the grossest materialistic conception, that the mind is the product of the body, we should expect to find the completest correspondences therefore between them. Or, to take the reverse of the picture, if we assume that the mind fashions the body we arrive, irresistibly, at a similar conclusion. The hand, physically, has been the instrument of man's emergence from the brute kingdom. By virtue of its capacity to grasp a weapon, a tool, a pen, a brush, man has become like unto the gods, knowing good and evil. Is it to be wondered at, therefore, that the hand from one point of view and the brain from another should provide an index to his character and a meter of his capacity ?

Broadly, the use of the hand in certain avocations leads to the presentation of certain characteristics. It is not a very wide guess to surmise that a person possessing energy and perseverance should have firm and well-defined hands. A careless, idle, thoughtless life, too, would conceivably not be without its power to leave an impress on the hands

174

of the subject. These would be only the broadest of indications. But taken in conjunction with other indexes, they would be valuable and trustworthy. That the lines in the hand, also, do really coincide with certain evidences of particular careers, incidents and accidents, is also undeniable. It is only when, to dependable indications of general character, fanciful and decorative details are added which cannot legitimately be deduced, that palmistry becomes an obvious example of chicanery.

Perhaps the best support that can be adduced for palmistry is to take the impressions of the hands of well-known individuals and to construct from them a reading in accordance with the principles of the art. The current issue, as we write, of the *International Psychic Gazette* gives detailed delineations, by C. W. Child, of the hands of three eminent scientists. In addition to an almost meticulous analysis of all the principal characteristics, intellectually, psychologically and temperamentally, of each individual, there are comparisons of the differences, similarities and coincidences of the indications on which the readings are based. The same principles and measures of signification are used. But the variety of effect in detail is well-nigh bewildering.

This is because the hand, as was suggested, must be read as a co-ordinated whole. Each indication must be considered in relation to all the others which modify it by their interaction. Palmistry, like other arts, is not the acquisition of a day. Its alphabet may be gleaned in an hour; but the capacity to assert, to weigh, to compare and synthesise the infinitesimally varying values of the multitude of signs, is to be acquired only by persistent study and effort directed to that end over a very long period. This is why, as was stated in the opening paragraph of this chapter, it is possibly the least reputable of the arts. Most of those who practise it are unqualified quacks. They have seen in its easily acquired " patter " a means to earn easy money. They have counted upon the wholesale credulity of the human being and his inordinate curiosity. They are pretenders and usurpers, and they must not be confused with those reputable practitioners who have devoted years to the study of the art, basing their ultimate practice upon classified data as

176

reliable as those of the other so-called exact sciences. Palmistry, in their hands, must be accredited a true art, because it also has satisfied the pragmatic test. It works.

But, in addition to the empirical method of delineation, founded mainly on cheirosophy, there is the intuitively assisted method. This was referred to earlier. There are many natural psychics. They do not consciously practise occult arts, nor do they knowingly depend upon their natural capacity to exercise telepathy and clairvoyance. They just do it. This is undoubtedly the case with many Gypsies, instances of whose wonderful powers are recorded. Whilst ostensibly reading the lines of the palm, its contours and the conformation of the hand, they are actually guided by information received unconsciously through the psychic or etheric senses.

Their wild free life allows ample opportunities for the development of the imaginative faculties. They read unknowingly the astral records. They sense the thoughts, desires and aspirations of their clients. The wish is father to the thought. True. And yet truer is it that the thought *is* the life. As we think, so we become. We are often the

12

wholly unconscious arbiters of our own fates. We will, and we find that we are. This, of course, refers more particularly to those who are thinkers, and not mere drifters. The former are creators. The latter mere mirrors which reflect the beams which momentarily fall upon them. Those who think creatively stir the astral atmosphere vitally and forcibly, and easily impress the natural psychic.

As to the fundamental reasons why certain indications should always be associated with specific characters, no explanation is possible. We find, experimentally and experientially, that it is so, and must be satisfied with that. If the hands of a dozen, or a hundred, persons be examined, who have led a fairly healthy life up to old age, certain lines will be found invariably which coincide with the principles of the science.

This experience may be repeated indefinitely. The more hands we examine and compare, the greater becomes the strength of the evidence for its validity. The " how " and the " why " may evade us, but we can at least make use of the information afforded. We do not really know how light waves are propagated in the ether. We do not know why light waves of a certain wave-length always give rise to a certain sensation of colour in our consciousness. But we know that they always do so, and we act accordingly. So too with palmistry. A detailed reading will afford a wealth of information which is valuable.

The Socratic axiom as to the necessity for, and advantage of, self-knowledge is yet true. Few are capable of such detached self-examination and analysis as palmistry, in the hands of a capable exponent, affords, by a careful delineation. Tendencies and characteristics may be modified and altered and transformed by self-education. But one has to be aware first that alterations are desirable. And usually we fail to distinguish our own weaknesses. We are not always conscious, either, of our strength. Strength may be made of more service to us if properly understood and consciously directed. Weaknesses may be controlled and eliminated when we know them for what they are and endeavour to right them.

CHAPTER XI

OMENS AND ORACLES

DIVINATION by omens or oracles is one of
the oldest of the occult arts. Like astrology,
it has been, in some periods of historic time,
upheld by the State, and officially practised
in its interest. The College of Augurs at
Rome will occur at once to the classical
student. He will need, perhaps, less remind-
ing of the prominence of the oracles in the
Grecian epoch. A little further back we have
the Egyptian oracles. To-day, in the extension of our knowledge of anthropology and
folklore, we note how widespread has been
the practice of observing omens and consulting
oracles in almost every phase of intellectual
growth.

Astronomical phenomena were the basis of
astrological science. The separate incidents
were noted as omens ; as portents generally
180

of evil. Man in his primitive state was obsessed with fear. Hence his prognostications were usually of woe and distress. As he grew in knowledge and learned to conquer the powers of nature, he was enabled to see in unusual happenings the indications also of good fortune to come. Dreams and apparitions were held to be of profound significance. Though many dreams might have been accounted for by aberrations of the physiological processes, there was a residue in which indications were given of future events. That such is the case to-day, no serious student of psychology denies. The instances are too many, and too well vouched to be explicable on the score of coincidence. Dreams, then, formed an important factor in the field of omens.

Dreaming itself is a passive function. The faculties are not normally exercised in dreaming. Two points arise from this consideration. Because volition is not exercised in dreaming, the experiences are frequently not sequential, nor orderly. As a result it was found that it was necessary to have an interpretation of the dreams if their significance was to be fully understood. Hence arose the need for divination by seers who would explain the import of the dreams.

Thus it is seen that though dreaming itself is not an occult art any more than mediumship is, divination, for purposes of interpretation, is an occult art. The materialistically inclined will perhaps say that the seeing of apparitions and visions are merely a daydreaming. " Such stuff as dreams are made of " readily recurs. But this is to beg the question now, when it is generally scientifically admitted that dreams, even, are an indication of consciousness on another plane of being. The student of psychic processes sees in dreaming a real functioning, though this is mostly aimless and inconsequent. There is usually, too, an extreme difficulty in bringing over to the waking consciousness the result of the astral perambulations.

This is not unreasonable. We should not expect a child of quite tender years to be able to reconstruct and relate its experiences of travel through strange lands and contact with strange peoples. It would have hazy notions of dimly perceived differences. But these would be inchoate and unreal to it by comparison with the solidity of its normal

182

surroundings. And so it is with dreams.
We are children of tender years. Our astral
senses are imperfectly awakened to the
perceptions. Our notions are dim and hazy.
And when we recall them at all it is as a mere
confused mass of impressions which we dis-
perse as idle chimera.

But there comes a time when the visions
are no longer blurred, indefinite and confusing.
They assume sharply defined characters and
lines. There is an intensity of impression
that carries the ideas clearly over into the
waking consciousness. There is an actuality
and a reality in the perceptions which will
no longer be denied. The child has grown.
The senses are attuned more accurately to the
vibrations. What is seen and heard is understood and takes form accordingly. The astral
senses are awakening to the new world in
which the wanderer has blundered and
stumbles. " Behold I dreamed a dream."

It was held, for ages, that dreams, or dream
visions, were sent from above as warnings.
It was the simplest form of communication
between the Divine and His creatures. The
ordinary mortal could not face directly the
glory of the divine. Its voice could be heard

and its mandate given only when shrouded. Its supreme refulgence was too great for direct approach. The full vision would have been too awful to withstand. So, in the old scriptures, man was warned in a dream. Or when an apparition was necessary, the divine took shape of lowlier mien. An angel appeared—Jacob wrestled with the angel. Later there were the burning bush, the cloud by day and the pillar of fire by night. Dreams and apparitions were the forerunners of omens and oracles. Perhaps the first instance recorded of the former would be the voice of God as He walked in the garden with His threat of evil as the punishment for man's disobedience.

Prophecy, both sacred and profane, was more akin to omen than to oracle. The essential difference between them would appear to be that an omen is unsought. It occurs, and its meaning has to be assigned. The oracle, on the other hand, is consulted when it is desired to read the future. Omen and oracle are complement and supplement. The oracle was devised to supply the blanks left by omens.

The prophets of old were leaders of the

184

people. By their apparent capacity to read signs and portents ; because of their ability to read the future and direct the movements, social, moral and political of their flocks; leadership was tacitly given them. They spoke out of the fullness of their knowledge. They communed with the oversoul. They were enabled to observe and read the signs which were not seen by others. They constructed a view of the future from the higher vision accorded them. Their astral senses were awake. They used the knowledge thus gleaned to advise and abjure the peoples they led. And from their prophecies arose a record which time has justified over and over again as if to confuse and confute beforehand those who would deny the possibilities of such foreknowledge.

And so long as modern thought confined itself to the realm of the purely physical, to that which could be weighed in the balance, or measured in velocity, it was incredulous and condemnatory. But now that the psychical is at least receiving attention, and the physical has receded over the borders of ethereality, justification is at hand for prophecy.

185

Omens may be roughly divided into two classes, particular and general. In the former are to be found those which, while not applicable invariably to a single individual, are yet of a personal character. The spectral coach, which is reported to drive up to the door of a North-country mansion and presages a death in the family, is one. The white bird of the Oxenhams, which has given warnings for generations, is another. The Banshee, of Highland tradition, which is heard by members of the family as a summons to one of them to prepare to depart, is a further instance of the particular case of omens.

Allied to this type of omen is that of the luck of Edenhall, the statue of Pallas at Troy, the coronation stone of Scone, and the Ancile. Each of these possessions, whilst it was retained in the hands of those who owned them, assured them of success. But their loss or destruction presaged disaster. When the wooden statue of Pallas at Troy was stolen by the Greeks the city was reduced and fired. The removal of the coronation stone to Westminster carried with it the succession to the throne of Scotland. Rome fell when its Palladium was lost.

186

A well-authenticated case of personal omen is that of a family in which, three days before the death of a member, a dirge-like strain of music is heard in the air. This, according to tradition, has been observed for centuries. One member of the family who had heard it himself twice, and noted the accuracy of its forebodings, attempted to discover its origin.

It appeared that in the twelfth century the head of the family took with him to the crusades his youngest and favourite son. The son was killed in battle. The father lamented his untimely and unprepared death. So great, indeed, was his grief that, returning to England, he entered one of the monastic orders. His purpose was twofold. He desired to spend the remainder of his life in prayer—first, for the repose of the soul of his son ; secondly, that in future no descendant of his should meet his fate without due time for preparation. For years his most intense desires were concentrated upon the fulfilment of his purpose.

The occultist would explain the result by the formation of an agency with nature spirits, or elementals, which would persist for untold generations, by virtue of the activity and intensity of the thought power poured into the astral atmosphere. The form of the agency was of no concern to the pious crusader. He was intent only that his warning should be heard. As thought is a persistent force, or mode of energy, it was concentrated with the elementary powers and is liberated now as occasion arises. The direct descendants of the old crusader hear again the strains of martial music which was the dirge in Palestine seven hundred years ago.

Many similar cases could be cited. And it would probably be found that most of them are explicable on the same lines. The records of the great families teem with these personal warnings or omens. However absurd it may be considered is the apparent credulity of those who take them as warnings, they have the justification to urge that they work. The warnings are generally true prognostications. And what more could one ask ?

But quite apart from these individual and personal indications are omens of general significance. These are multifarious. The breaking of a picture cord, the violent slamming of a door, when there is no draught to cause it, breaking a mirror, stumbling or

188

falling, the crossing of the path by a black cat, the creaking of furniture, the appearance of an owl or its screeching, the flight or fighting of birds, spilling the salt, howling of dogs, ear-tingling, all are general omens of various import. These are general omens which are known to most Western peoples as popular superstitions.

Each land has its own variants of their significance in detail. But there is a striking similarity and agreement almost on the main points of the values of each omen. It would seem that there has been either a common source from which such knowledge or myth has been derived, or that there is some under-lying principle to which they may be referred. It would be difficult to justify the former pro-position,—and not much less so, perhaps, to elucidate the truth of the second.

In India, the land of magic and mystery, omens form no small part of the religious beliefs of many of the peoples. For India, be it remembered, is an agglomeration of races, nations and tribes. In no other part of the world, possibly, are we able to trace such profound distinctions in language, customs, economics and morality. But underlying it all is the dependence upon omens. Reference is made in the Hindu classics to omens associated with quiverings and throbbings of the body. A quivering of the right eye indicates good luck. A quivering sensation in the right arm is believed to denote marriage with a beautiful woman.

In offering animal sacrifices, a practice still maintained in many parts of India, the movements of the animal before the slaughter are carefully observed. A very liberal interpretation is placed upon the slightest movement. A voluminous list of omens is given, both good and bad, as observed in Malabar. Crows and pigeons, moving from left to right, and dogs and jackals moving in the reverse directions, are accounted good. Screams, cursing, sneezing, a stool carried with its legs upwards, or a cup or dish carried with its mouth downwards, is bad. The worst of all omens is allowing a cat to cross one's path. On New Year's Day, the effect of omens is believed to last for the ensuing year.

If a winnow slips when winnowing rice, or the oven gives vent to a hissing noise, the arrival of a guest is foreshadowed. If a light goes out during meals, it is an evil omen. If a traveller sees a hare on his way he will not succeed in the object of his journey. When a child sneezes the bystanders wish it long life. Eclipses are periods of evil. Comets are also evil omens. A third wedding is considered to be of evil import amongst the Brahmans. If a Brahman, therefore, desires to marry a third wife, he is first wedded to a tree, the arka plant. The third wife then becomes his by a fourth marriage, and so the evil omen is averted.

There is a Tamil proverb relating to the selection of a wife, to the effect that curly hair gives food, thick hair brings milk, and very stiff hair destroys a family. Omens in connection with child-bearing and birth are numerous and curious. The birth of a Korava child on a new moon night is an omen that it will have a notorious thieving future. If a dog scratches the wall of a house it will be broken into by thieves. A dog approaching a person with a bit of shoe leather augurs success. If a dog enters a house with wire in its mouth, the master of the house must expect to be put in prison.

The hair marks on the bodies of horses and oxen, formed by the changes of direction in which the hair is growing, called the crown, ridge or feather mark, form the criterion of its value. The positions indicate whether the animal will bring luck or not to its owner ; an animal is rarely kept which has unlucky marks. For much of this information on India, the present writer is indebted to Mr Edgar Thurston's work, entitled *Omens and Superstitions of Southern India.*

It would be well-nigh hopeless to attempt to give a specific explanation of each of the omens to which reference has been made. It must be sufficient to try to prove a general justification for them. But first it is desirable to refer to the degradation of idea which almost invariably occurs with the lapse of time, and by the passage of a notion, orally, through successive generations. As a platitude, the saying that there is no smoke without fire is hard to beat. And its most useful analogy, perhaps, is that there is no myth without truth. The foundation of all myth is doubtless historical fact in every instance. But so distorted and overloaded does it become, that it is sometimes difficult to trace its origin or to recognise its validity.

So with many omens. Starting with an

actual occurrence, possibly with a tragic termination, there was a linking of cause and effect. Phenomena occurring concurrently with or immediately before the happening were ascertained to have something to do with its causation. The connection at times quite conceivably may have been remote. But like circumstances being thought invariably to produce like effects, it would be recorded amongst the wise ones that such things were of evil import.

In other words, the basis of the belief in omens is experience. And, lest it be urged by the dialectical that superstition might be similarly defended, let it be said at once that this is equally true. The grossest superstition has its origin in fact. It may be difficult to deduce the fact from which it arises, but it is nevertheless true that the most absurd— apparently—superstitions have actually arisen in this way.

Witchcraft, sorcery, and magic, to mention three only of what it is common to call superstitions, are now known to all serious students to have a very real basis in natural, but frequently perverted, powers. There is no supernatural. The supernormal there may be, and is. The piety which believes in the miracles of Christ, and the bigotry which ascribes sorcery to the devil, are not far wide of the mark.

A better understanding of the underlying principles of the universe has shewn how futile were our previously limited concepts. The supernormal tends constantly to become the normal. The boundaries of the physical plane are being pushed outwards. We begin to sense the psychical, the ethereal, the mental and the spiritual planes, which lie beyond it and behind it. We begin daily to realise that the physical plane is a mere cloak, that it is but a garment of manifestation, for the powers which reside beyond its valuations, to use for their projections.

There is no breaking of the natural laws in miracles. There is but the extension of those laws in a supernormal exhibition of the ultimate spiritual energy which is the essence of the universe and the cause of its appearance. The stilling of the storm, the resurrection of the body, the thousandfold reproduction of the loaves and fishes, are marvellous exhibitions, but are not even the transcendence of natural law. They are explicable by the dicta

194

of modern science. They are not to be reproduced by Tom, Dick or Harry. But they
are neither impossibilities nor distortions of
facts. They are simply revelations of the
mastery of the higher principles over the
lower forms which depend upon them.

Matter, that wonderful sheet anchor of
physical science, is in the last analysis only
the ether in motion. The physical atom is
the universe in microcosm; within it resides
an almost unbelievable store of energy. It is,
in fact, just a centre of energy.

But thought, the servant or vehicle of the
will, is another form of energy. Hypnotic
phenomena shew this to be so. The physical
is subservient to, dependent upon, the psychical. The tiny magnet of the school child
will lift a little piece of steel or iron, weighing
a few grammes. The modern electrical gen-
erator, the huge alternating machine, will
hurl at a tremendous speed masses weighing
a million times as much. The principle is
the same, the power is identical. It is only
a difference in the quantity of the energy used.
The thought, then, which will induce a
muscular contraction in the limb of the
hypnotised subject is capable too of producing

meteorological changes; changes in the polarity of the atoms of the human body; dissociation of material bodies; association of material bodies.

Man, essentially, is a dynamo. But usually he acts as a motor only. Rarely is he dynamic. He is respondent rather than originative. He is a standing example of the physical convertibility of electrical machines. They may be used, by the application of current to them, to produce mechanical motion. By the application of mechanical motion to them they may be made to produce electrical energy. In his response to the grosser influences man is the motor. He gives out mechanical energy only.

By linking himself up with the basic spiritual force of the universe, he becomes capable of output of vast stores of electrical energy. He becomes dynamic. He shews a potentiality for good or evil of immense range and almost inconceivable power. The Christ was just such a dynamo. By virtue of His association with the Father, the typified oversoul, as the vehicle of the ultimate spiritual energy of the universe, He was able to manifest that power in various ways. His was the gigantic system of electrical alternators which could produce a storm as easily as still it, which could dissociate His own body or cause it to appear, as readily as He was able to multiply, to produce, in fact, bread and fish from the ethereal world stuff from which all materiality arises.

Omniscience bears to supernormal premonition much the same relation that the alternator does to the child's magnet. All men are potential Christs. But the day of entering completely into their kingdom is afar off. Many, however, begin to shew signs that the gulf is not impassable. They realise themselves, and serve to shew to others, that there is a gradation of power which leads, little by little, to omnipotence. There is the possibility of getting into perceptual contact with the oversoul which, in its fullest commingling, is what we should conceive as practical omniscience. "The Father and I are one," said the Christ. And this because His union with the source of all things was complete. The most highly developed men fall far short of even a remote approach to such magnificence.

But there is promise in the words, " Be ye

therefore perfect even as the Father which is in Heaven is perfect." The way is indicated. " Seek ye first the Kingdom." These are the words of a mystic. They must be interpreted mystically. There must be a cultivation of those internally carried powers. There must be an opening of the higher centres of being to the finer pulsations from the spiritual fount of life. The ego, the higher self, must be awakened to the impulses from above and beyond. Then there will be a stirring of the perceptions.

Then, instead of misty notions dimly perceived to bear some little relation to coming events, there will be a fuller, wider knowledge of what is to befall. The distorted suggestiveness of omens will be replaced by a conscious preparation for the future, which will be determined and foreknown by the actions of the present.

CHAPTER XII

CONCLUSION

A BRIEF survey may now be permitted in which to review, as a summary, the propositions made in the foregoing chapters, and the arguments used to defend and support the propositions. A very wide field has been opened, and it has not been possible to do more than just touch the matter at various points. But the aim has always been to avoid mere polemic. It has been the writer's endeavour to keep in fairly close contact with the dicta of modern scientific research. For this purpose to be effected it was desirable to restrict the treatment of each subject to the barest outlines, and then to compare it with its physical opponent; for modern science was until quite recently almost wholly concerned with the physical and materialistic side of the universe. And, if not actually positive in its denial of the psychic and spiritual side, it had adopted an attitude of supercilious agnosticism.

But its own inertia, the result of its unwisely rapid progress on the physical side, has carried it, in its conclusions, beyond its own borders. It has burnt its ships. Matter, to which it pinned its hope, as its sheet anchor, has been destroyed by its own analysis. The physical terms, in which it used to dogmatise and postulate so freely, have come to possess little significance. Mass, time, distance, velocity and inertia have been superseded, by the reduction of that which exhibited these functions to its primal base, by an ether, of hypothetical rather than actual existence, of apparently profoundly contradictory attributes. But out of the mass of apparent contradictions has arisen a pabulum of doctrine which is sufficiently precise and rational to meet our needs. It is, however, largely metaphysical rather than scientific. Perhaps ultra-scientific would be the better word. And it is this ultra science which supports our claims.

Throughout the series it has been shewn that for many of the occult arts, evidence is available of its practice right through the historical period. The practice, indeed, of magic arts is as old as mankind itself. For there have always been inequalities in the degree of growth attained at any particular period. There have always been some of the race who have been ahead of the great mass in perception of the finer forces of nature. These, making use of their crudely handled and dimly ascertained knowledge, have exercised domination over their fellows. Whether it be one of the magi of Persia or the Voodooist of the African tribes, the religious ecstasist of the twentieth century or the necromancer of the twentieth century of the pre-Christian era, the omen diviner of to-day or of forty centuries ago, the astrologer of Babylon or of Bond Street, each in his turn, and in his time, has secured the adhesion of his following.

There has never been a time in history when the occult arts were not known and practised. Their antiquity, then, cannot be gainsaid. And they were, and are, equally ubiquitous ! There is no land—from China to Peru—where such arts have not been always known and practised. From the Shaman of the Esquimaux to the witch doctor and medicine man of the antipodean aborigines, there is no hiatus. Malay, Mongol, Caucasian, Ethiopian and Negro, all contribute their quota of evidence. This being so, it would be unreasonable to dismiss such voluminous and corroborative evidence as having no basis in fact. It may be distorted and deformed. It may be unclean and unwholesome. It may be undignified and immoral. It may be diabolic. But it exists, and has existed for all the historical ages, in all climes, as a belief that there are abnormal powers and there are those who have as constantly exercised them.

A good case had therefore been made out for the examination of these claims, and a start was made with Alchemy. This was dealt with first because our impressions begin with the world of sensation. Man, like all the other physical organisms, responds to stimuli. These, raining on him from without, are the cause, immediately, of all that he is and does. Like the lowliest organisms, man is tropistic. He turns to the sun. His physical life is an interaction of forces. Chemical action leads to mechanical action.

CONCLUSION

Chemical action, in metabolism, is the basis of physical existence.

It was fitting, therefore, that alchemy, the parent of the science by virtue of which man, considered physically, is enabled to see, hear, touch, taste and smell, should receive the first consideration. Alchemy, it was shewn, is a belief in the unity of the primal substance from which the universe and man himself is formed, in the transmutability of any of its accidental and phenomenal appearances, and in the possibility of immortality for man, as typifying the universe. Man, through the ages, sought to discover the laws of association and dissociation of matter, and under a cloak of symbolism veiled his processes so that the profane might be kept from the secret and sacred knowledge he pursued.

Alchemy was both physical and spiritual. Physical in so far as the object of the quest was the reduction of one element to its base and the reproduction of another in its stead. Spiritual, because the physical processes were seen to be the outward forms of an internally perceived noumenon. The physical alchemist sought to make his lead into gold. The spiritual alchemist desired a similar change for the gross nature of man to become the Divine.

Gold is not yet produced by physical process from lead. Nor has man yet achieved the transmutation of his sensuous nature into Divinity. But the claims of alchemy, nevertheless, stand quite justified. The underlying principles upon which the postulates were founded have been substantiated. The basis of matter, the material of gold and of lead, the substance of which each is a differing form, has been admitted to be homogeneous world stuff.

There is no essential difference in electrons. They are the fundamental submaterial basis of physical-sense matter. Mass and motion have been deposed. Energy and ether reign instead. The king is dead. Long live the king. The terms are changed, but the ultimate concepts remain. The thing moved, and that which moves it, are the sole realities. And from one point of view the two are one —the eternally manifesting spirit - substance which is the ever - becoming. Ether and stress-energy are the duality available for our primal cognisance. The ultimate unity is incomprehensible.

CONCLUSION

Ether in a state of stress is cognisable as the electron. The aggregation of electrons produces the atom of the element. Diversity of grouping of the electrons gives rise to the physical properties of the various elements. In essence the elements are one. The mother-nature basically is homogeneous. Gold is lead under another form. The substance is the same, but the form is the vehicle of transcience. The apparently indestructible elements of matter are now admitted to be changing modes of electron-groups. All matter is more or less radio-active. No form of matter is permanent. It is in process of change as we view it. Its dissolution is proceeding as we haste to qualify it.

That alchemical transmutation is now not generally effected as a physical process, counts for little. That it is possible is certain. That it will be effected is to be anticipated. That it has always been possible has been demonstrated. So that the alchemists were in the right in their speculations in this direction. In another field, too, their quest is receiving strong support. The search for the elixir of life was also not so absurd as has seemed to be the case. The experiments of an eminent bacteriologist and biologist, Dr Carel, of New York, have shewn that isolated fragments of living tissue may be made to pass through processes of rejuvenation.

The normal life-cycle may be repeated almost indefinitely by cleansing the fragments of organism and altering its food stuff. This, as a chemical process of metabolism, is closely akin to the successful demonstration of the immortality in the flesh, of the completer organism, man. The cleansing process, too, which is imperative if the rejuvenation is to be successful, is suggestive. It is allied to the spiritual, alchemical change which was necessary in the constitution of man's moral nature. The change had to be radical and complete. There was to be a polarisation of principle. The direction of the motive was to be altered. There was to be a transmutation of desire.

Spiritual regeneration of this kind is not unknown. It is a fact of experience. The change is a vivid and thorough one. There is a washing, a cleansing of the system, and a redirected objective. The goal is changed. The mode of life is changed. The man is changed. There has been effected a real transmutation. The three chief claims of the alchemists, then, have been triumphantly vindicated. And physics, biology, and psychology have been the witnesses for the defence whose evidence has established a verdict for the appellant.

Astrology was the second of the occult arts to be brought to the bar for judgment. And this because arising out of the particular sense impressions, which are seen to be the basis of our knowledge, are those more general observations of the larger bodies, the celestial bodies, which we can know less intimately. The sense channels through which they can affect us are fewer. But their mobility and the profundity of the distances they connote make a larger appeal to us. Unchanging apparently in substance, their motion is apparent even to casual observation.

They would thus give rise to general notions of a more abstract character than the smaller things close at hand. They would form a subject for close study to some minds. Coincidences of events of unusual character with special conjunctions of the heavenly bodies would be noted. A correspondence would be assumed between the celestial occurrences and those in human affairs. Data would be accumulated. And on this would be erected a superstructure of empirical science.

Hypothesis would in time be superseded by theory, which, tested and tried by fresh experiences, would evolve into material of reasonable exactitude. From the more isolated instances of correspondence between event and celestial movements would arise the theory of the virtual determination of character and temperament by the positions and interactions of the heavenly bodies on the human constitution. Terrestrial phenomena would be assigned to celestial influence. The science of astrology would then flower in all its glory.

As it would be possible to predict the positions of the celestial bodies, it would be possible also to predict the changes of the individual affected thereby. In addition, therefore, to the determination of general characteristics and dispositions, it would be possible to predict the eventful phases which would occur in the life-cycle of the individual.

Now the general justifications for the validity of the claims of astrology rest upon meteorology and astrophysics and upon psychology in its aspect of physiological-psychological parallelism. Meteorology has shewn that there is a very real correspondence between the physical phenomena of the weather and celestial influences. The sun is undoubtedly of the most vital importance in the determination of the weather. Of little less importance is the moon. The planetary influences, in exact science, are less clearly defined. But the modern meteorologist is beginning to realise that conjunctions and oppositions of the planets have a bearing upon the weather.

Astrophysics have enabled us to trace heat and electro-magnetic disturbances to such remote distances as the stars represent. The physical influences of differing rays and differing emanations continuously and variably affect us, man, physically. Astrology, therefore, considered as a physical science, is quite justified. It is when we leave the sphere of the purely physical and enter that of the psychical that we begin to encounter difficulties.

But these difficulties vanish on examination. For psychology itself expounds the doctrine of parallelism. It asserts that there is no change of mental state without its cor-

14

responding change in physiological base. Conversely this must also be true. A change in the physiological condition must also be accompanied by a change in the psychic processes. If, then, it be granted that the celestial bodies can, and do, affect us physically, they also can, and must, affect us psychically. The degree of perceptive consciousness to the influences may be little. We may not recognise that it has affected us at all. But we have to consider, now, that the stimuli which rain upon us, without consciously affecting us, may nevertheless be affecting us all the time.

Light rays, for example, to which we are constantly subjected, are only perceived by the vision for a tiny fraction of their complete range. Sound vibrations, too, only affect us consciously within a very limited range. But all the vibrations, above and below the scale we sense, are capable of affecting us, and we are justified in believing that they do so. The ultra violet light rays have a great capacity for dissociation of chemical compounds. The use of concentrated rays shews their dissociative power when they are applied to the human body. And it may quite well be that sound

210

vibrations which we cannot hear have also the power to affect us.

It would be unwise, therefore, to deny that because we are not directly aware of the effect of such influences that they do not exist. The electro-magnetic forces of the sun and planets and the stars may quite conceivably be able to disturb the constitution of the human body, if we but reflect a moment. In ultimate analysis the human body is a quivering, vibrating structure of electrons. The electrons are merely stressed ether. The oscillating waves of energy, proceeding from the giant bodies in space, sweep on and on, and we are included in their range.

An electric storm in the sun affects our terrestrial magnetism. But magnetism is but a form of electrical energy. Man is but a magnet. And the storm that affects the earth affects him also. Differences in physical constitution may, after all, be only differences in electrical potential. The basic equilibrium may be less in one than in another. The storm that will completely change the polarity of one system may merely affect a small deviation of polar-angularity in another. But then these physical changes are those which in psychological parallelism are allied to changes in mental process. The increase or decrease in electrical stress effects a similar disturbance on the mental plane. All matter is radio-active. The human body falls within the universal. It also is radio-active. The celestial bodies are so also.

There must, therefore, be an interchange of material between the most remote bodies in space. Astrology postulates such interchanges. It has built upon this a hypothesis of specific influences for each of the important celestial bodies individually. It subjects its hypothesis to test. It answers the test successfully. Again and again it tries, and with each successful essay the truth of its theory is the more firmly established. It has built up for itself a pragmatic sanction. For astrology works.

Passing then to psychometry, it was suggested that material objects could be so impressed with the stress of a thought current that, given the necessary conditions, such stress could be recovered and reproduced in the ideation of the sensitive. The implication made was that thought is a force. It was stated that thought possesses the power of changing the state of rest or motion of a body. That this is so must be granted. For thought is not material in the ordinary sense of the word.

Neither materialist nor idealist would assert that thought is material. And since the ordinary categories allow us finally only to choose between matter and motion, or electrons and energy, thought, if not material, must be a form of energy. The idealist would concede the point at once. The materialistic scientist would hedge. He might say, he has said, that thought is a function of matter. But since inertia is the root, or essential, attribute of matter, motion cannot well arise from that which is, in itself, inherently, and positively, inert or motionless. The source or cause of motion—energy itself —must necessarily, and eternally, be outside matter.

It is merely begging the question to suggest, as M. Gustave Le Bon does in his *Evolution of Matter,* that matter itself is the boundless store from which energy is derived. That matter contains boundless stores of energy, interatomically, is undoubtedly true. But since we distinguish between matter and energy, as we all do, the fact that energy is found associated with matter, but is released by the dissociation of matter, is the best ground for assuming that the association of the two in the first place is that which gives rise to the phenomena of matter, and the withdrawal of energy is that which permits the primal substance to reassume its original status as non-matter world stuff, or matter *in potentio* only.

Matter, then, is a store of energy only because the energy has associated with itself this potential world stuff. The energy of matter can be released by dissociation only because it has first been combined. The two, ether and energy, are always, both as agent and principal, to be distinguished. They are mutually exclusive. The one is not a product or function of the other. They are partners or adversaries according to how we view them. It is energy, then, that binds the electron into the atom. It is energy which binds the atom into the molecule. Energy plays its part, too, in the association of the larger aggregates.

Thought, then, if not material, must be immaterial. And since it is a real something, which does something, it must fall within the

214

other category, of force, or that which tends to change a body's state of rest or motion. Thought, therefore, is that which changes the form, or arrangements, of the grey matter of the brain. It is a real force capable of doing work—and doing it.

In one of the latter chapters man has been compared with a dynamo. He is constantly producing and throwing off electrical energy. The pressure varies. In some cases the potential is very high. In others, by comparison, the potential is low. Thought currents vary in intensity. There is the thought winged with power to kill. There is the other thought that swings idly round in the astral plane, banged and buffeted by virtue of its helplessness. The highly dynamic thought impresses itself as a definite and specific stress upon the vibrating and oscillatory particles and aggregates which constitute matter.

This action has been compared with that of the concentrated rays of light upon a sensitised plate, which awaits the action of the developer to reveal the latent image. The psychometrist fills the gap. His finer senses enable him to perceive the impressed stress. Like the bloodhound, he is able to differentiate between the numberless other indications offered. His action is selective and recreative. He reconstructs the scene, more or less accurately, as his perceptions allow. His etheric senses have to be trained to perceive and collate and re-present, just as the normal senses have to be trained. His misconceptions are similar. His mistakes and errors are due to the same cause : the lack of experience to arrange, classify, and analyse and synthesise his perceptions.

The capacity of the psychometrist to detect the nature of material which is not directly amenable to his ordinary senses is probably due to the perception and recognition of its emanations. All matter being more or less radio-active, it is constantly pouring off streams of particles which are electronic rather than atomic. These correspond fairly closely to the material vehicles of the next plane—the astral—that through which the etheric senses of the psychometrist function. The emanations produce such changes as enable them to be sensed in this manner.

In telepathy was seen the extension of the arguments given above. Thought being a force is capable of influencing, and does influence, the material particles of the brain substance of others. It awakens in them, when they are attuned to receive them, vibrations and rearrangements of the brain matter which, parallelism assures us, connotes thought perceptions received from outside, and not directly arising as the result of reflective and associative processes. The transmission of human thought is no more marvellous than wireless telegraphy. In fact there is a great similarity between them. The mechanism employed is almost identical. The brain is the alternating machine producing the sparks of high voltage and rapid frequency—the thoughts—which, impelled into space, radiate equally all round through the ether.

When the electric waves are intercepted by the coherer the local circuit is closed. In telepathy this means that the thought currents are intercepted by a coherer—another brain attuned to respond, because of its consciously directed polarisation of brain material. The local circuit is then closed. The brain of the recipient is energised by the thought currents impinging upon it. The relay then operates. The stimulation of the brain material is transformed into perception, or ideation, and the message is taken down, transcribed or reproduced on the sounder.

For the successful transmission of thought the two principal instruments must be well equipped for the purpose. The thoughts to be transmitted must be consciously produced with that intention in view ; they must be consciously concentrated, or focussed, and despatched definitely, and with determination, to reach their mark. Similarly, the recipient must be passively attentive, with organised brain material, awaiting the impulses which will stir the grey matter to activity.

It seems quite unnecessary to labour the point that etheric vibrations of any sort do actually result in correlative sensation, perception and ideation in the mind. Whatever the source of the vibration, the reaction inevitably follows. And this is also true of the vibrations of lower pitch in a denser medium. Sound vibrations, travelling through the air, are able to affect material of the same character, on the same plane so to speak, to respond. The vibration of a violin string will produce similar vibrations in all the material substances within its range if their specific character will permit them to vibrate at all. The human voice has the same capacity. The brain, used as an instrument for cerebration, produces thoughts. These are etheric vibrations. The vibrations are of higher pitch than sound-waves, and on another plane. They affect substance of a different order.

But just as the colour sensations, which are etheric vibrations, have to be evolved to be translated into perception and ideation, so has the capacity for perception of thoughts mentally transmitted from brain to brain to be evolved. In savage races of a low order of mentality, the colour sensations are very crude. There is no perception of the finer distinctions either of tint or tone. The sensations are quite rudimentary. The same holds good of thought transmission and perception. There is an absence of awareness. There is no finer sense organ as yet developed to catch the more subtle emanations. These vibrations fail to awaken the response.

But with those in whom the study of psychic activity has shewn the presence in the human organism of these higher centres of activity and response to stimuli, there is arising the capacity to transmit consciously to, and to receive thoughts from, other minds. The electrical analogy is the best that can be afforded. A strip of steel, freely suspended and rendered magnetic, is susceptible to the influence of an approaching magnetic field, or to the disturbance of an electric current, or wave. The brain which is sensitised, that is rendered magnetic by conscious polarisation, will perceive the thought currents projected in its direction. The mind, too, which, like the dynamo-electric machine, is organised for that purpose, has no difficulty in pouring out its electric waves, of varying pitch, frequency and intensity.

Proceeding, then, with clairvoyance, it was urged that this reputed power of inner sight, or sight at a distance, logically follows from the mere extension of the higher powers of the mind. The keynote, in fact, to the validity of clairvoyance is susceptibility to finer vibrations. The difference between the state of the conscious clairvoyant and the hypnotised subject is that the first-named produces by his own actions the condition desirable for the functioning of the higher centres.

There is such a wealth of reputable evidence for the truth of premonitions and of vision at a distance, that modern science, if unable to explain it, at least admits it as phenomena arising from an abnormal state of nervous activity. Hysteria and neurosis are states that favour these abnormal forms of mental activity. But it must be always remembered that parallelism is a fact in nature. Mental states or strains do result from physical stresses. And, conversely, physical stresses do result from mental strains.

Right thought connotes right action, and right action right thought. But what we are concerned with here more particularly is not the moral or ethical aspect of this abnormal nervous and mental activity, but its metaphysical aspect. Does it, or does it not obtain. Modern science, as said above, does not deny that it occurs. It merely pleads that it is the wrong action of the physical organism which produces aberration of the mental states. It vouches incidentally for the fact of the occurrences.

Now the visions of an epileptic may be neither comforting nor helpful. They may lead nowhere, nor be of use in vital evolution.

But in so far as they occur they prove the capacity of the human mind to exercise faculties of perception distinctly above and beyond the normal.

Clairvoyance is the conscious use of such faculties. It is not the result of an accidental stress which produces uncontrolled and undirected wanderings. But it is the volitional researches of a mind bent on gleaning in fresh fields of experience. The normal faculties being inhibited, there is an outreaching of the finer senses. The inner eye and ear are brought under control. The more delicate, the more subtle vibrations are entertained. There is a response to these finer stimuli. The etheric senses perceive dimly at first, and then more definitely, the larger world of experience and sensation opening to it.

Little material that is of value is to be obtained at first. Like the child, the clairvoyant has to co-ordinate his impressions and learn the meanings of things. There is frequent misapprehension. There are blunders and boggles. But out of the tangle arises some order. Chaos and nonentity begin to assume form and coherence. The new world has a meaning that is to be extracted by time and patience. Progress is slow. Each step in advance of the other is taken with fear if with deliberation. The explorer has to be wary. Pitfalls surround him on every side. He is in the terra incognita.

And the etheric world has its inhabitants. These regard the invasion of their sphere—as aboriginals in every other sphere regard it—as an unwarranted intrusion. There is opposition to progress. From this it may be inferred that the undirected roamings of the mentally unbalanced are difficult of comprehension. It may also help one to realise why the man of genius is usually erratic and eccentric. His excursions to the wonderland are frequently undertaken without conscious preparation or direction. He browses. The results of his reflections there are then communicated to a world which is only partially capable of following the flights he has taken.

Prophets and seers are clairvoyant. But they, like the other men of genius, are passive rather than active clairvoyants. The dreamer of dreams and the seer of visions are those who enter the kingdom of the—normally—unseen, without a plan or guide. They

have strayed in. They have made no organised attack on the inner world. The poet—
and most prophets are poets, and *vice versa*—
is also one who, in his commune with
nature, evades the world of grosser materiality, and fares forth to the other kingdoms.

His adventures, too, frequently shew the
flashes of his contact with the brighter realm
he has invaded all unconsciously. Glorious
are his visions : his views of a reconstructed
universe. These are his gleanings from the
world to be ; the world he sees unfolded to
his gaze. Merely the imaginings, says the
sceptic, of the disordered mind. But then
imagination is the power of the soul exer-
cising itself in creation. It is the planning
of that which is to emerge. The future is the
unfolding of the present. The present is but
the child of the past.

There is an illimitable, but immutable thread
spread through the eternities. We, in normal
vision, see at the moment but a tiny patch of
its pattern. With wider opened eyes we see
more and more of it. With the added vision
that clairvoyance gives it is possible to extend
that purview, back and forth, with a range
that steadily increases in intensity and defini-
224

tion, as the vision is evolved and consciously concentrated on that which it is desired to behold.

Following on with Spiritism, it was sought to shew that these etheric senses were the organs of a mechanism of more subtle character, of finer tenuity, than the physical body. The astral, or etheric shell, is material and composite, or at least organised, like that of the grosser material body of flesh, muscle, nerve and bone. This etheric shell remains for a time, like the physical body, a more or less completely organised structure after death has taken place on the physical plane. It is the persistence of this etheric double which has given rise to the evidence for phantasms of the dead. The clairvoyant is able to perceive this astral shell during the life of the individual, as a cloud of tenuous and filmy matter, interpenetrating and surrounding the physical body in a roughly ovoid shape.

At death, too, the clairvoyant perceives the severance of the two envelopes. The etheric or astral shape is seen to glide off from the presence of its grosser counterpart. Possibly no writer of fiction has more nearly approached the truth, as seen from the occult

15

standpoint, than H. G. Wells in some of his short stories. *Under the Knife,* for example, gives a realistic impression of the withdrawal of the consciousness from the physical body to the astral, and the wanderings of the latter through space, during the period of anæsthesia.

This, again, it will be said, is merely a matter of imaginative fiction. But Wells, like many other writers, in his wildest flights, apparently, gets nearest to the truth. And this because, by this power of detachment, he himself unconsciously has been in contact with the inner worlds of consciousness.

Evidence for the appearance of wraiths, spooks, ghosts, whatever we may be pleased to call them, is forthcoming in such abundance, variety and degree of corroboration, that it may be held that there is the same quality of proof for their existence as a fact in nature, as for the increase in temperature with a descent into the earth's crust, or for the differences in temperature between some of the remoter bodies in space. The evidence, as a whole, is probably stronger for the existence of phantasms than for the last dictum of science.

226

CONCLUSION

To take refuge in the statement that all such appearances of phantasms are abnormal is of little use. To the savage, unlearned in the arts and sciences of civilisation, the telephone and the incandescent gas or electric light are also abnormal. And, possibly, far more wonderful. The art of writing, and the phenomenon of the gramophone are almost beyond the range of human credulity in a simple state. The operations of the trained mind are little less wonderful to the more commonplace, but untaught individual.

Astrophysics may be taught to a board-school child. But he is wholly dependent upon his teachers. He has to accept as true what is taught, because the consensus of experience amongst a few observers has justified those conclusions. Only by the aid of delicately perceptive instruments are they able to observe the phenomena they analyse, synthesise and describe. Without those instruments, and without the aid of sympathetic hypotheses, they would be unable to proceed. Their progress would be barred.

Their instruments may be connoted to the higher degrees of susceptibility which the sensitive exhibits. For the phantasms are only to be seen by those whose sensitiveness is awakened. The differences in temperature between Arcturus and Sirius are not perceptible to the tissues of the hand which normally register such differences for us.

Spiritualistic phenomena have produced irrefutable evidence of the existence of the etheric double, or astral body, of the medium. The phenomena of materialisation is the best proof which could be desired of the existence of this substratum of the physical body. And although it may be admitted that séances have done little to prove the persistence of the astral after death, their evidence in another direction is valuable. Telepathy and clairvoyance are both proved by the séance. The medium, if actually unable to bring over fresh matter from the other side, has time and again seen and reproduced the knowledge of things known only to individual members of the circle.

In the trance condition there has been a perception of thought currents, and an inner vision, which, in their endeavour to prove the asserted communion with the dead, have demonstrated the existence and practice of the other occult faculties. In the opinion of

228

the present writer the séance defeats its own object by the employment of a medium, if it be desired to procure first-hand evidence of the persistence of the astral double after death. The practice of necromancy is strongly to be deprecated. It fulfils no useful purpose. It subjects those who affect it to the danger of temporary or even permanent obsession. And it hinders the progress of the entity passed over. At this we may well leave the subject.

In the chapter devoted to hypnotism the dominance of the mental impulse upon the material substance was shewn. The validity of psychological-physiological parallelism was plainly illustrated. The value of " suggestion," mental or verbal, was clearly indicated. It was seen to be a force in accordance with the concept of physical science. The thought of the operator was sufficient to secure movement in the subject. The varied phenomena of hypnotism and mesmerism are exceptionally valuable in a work seeking to establish the validity of the occult arts. The higher psychic activities, plainly discernible in hypnosis, are so well supported by scientific knowledge that for their acceptance no apologetics are necessary. Modern science does not refuse its sanction to the evidence largely collated and obtained by its own practitioners.

For those, then, to whom this little work is thought to be of too insufficient a character to justify all the conclusions of the writer, the literature which has grown around the subject of hypnotism and allied psychic phenomena generally is, therefore, recommended for perusal. Enough will be found there to point the way to further lines of research for first-hand evidence of the arts presented here in less detailed form. Hypnotism, indeed, may be said to present a synthetic foreground of the occult arts. It shews the possibilities of the latent faculties of man.

And though hypnotism may appear to be, superficially, but a physical process for the derangement of the normal faculties and the imposition of the will of another, inasmuch as it provides phenomena which far transcend normal experience, it proves for the operator, at least, what it may, perhaps, be held not to prove for the subject—that there are ranges of mental action quite beyond those exhibited by the ordinary individual.

Geomancy and palmistry, and divination by omens, carry the general arguments to their logical conclusions by diverse paths. Each depends upon the interpretation, by inner vision, of external indications or evidences. These external indications arise, it is held, in obedience to the law of causation. In geomancy, astrological data is utilised for the clothing of intuitive action with understandable formulæ. In palmistry the empirical data of cheirognomy, indicated by the hand itself, are interpreted by the seer in collaboration with the further assistance of clairvoyance and telepathy.

Each of the occult arts may be considered complementary and supplementary to the others. Omens, likewise, need the inner vision for their correct interpretation. Like the markings of the palm, and its general conformation, they provide rough approximations. The filling in of the blanks and the extension of the information thus sketchily provided is dependent upon the capacity of the exponent to make use of the higher faculties of the psychic senses.

Thus, starting with the concept of the unity and homogeneity of substance in alchemy, we are led to end upon a similar note of unison in synthesis. As in evolution we are permitted to cognise the emergence of energy and substance from the incomprehensible and eternal monad, and to watch its interplay in growing complexity of structure and diversity of form and function, so in devolution we may trace the possibilities of the return to simplicity and unity of all that is.

All is vanity. The aspirations and idealisations of the seer and prophet are seen to be but the workings, in their time and place, of the great breath which informs, animates, moves and supports, nay more, produces, the universe. The vibrating electron, the mighty solar system, the infinitesimal period of time we deem to be the thousandth part of a second, and the profoundly great cycles of sidereal time, reckoned in thousands of millions of years, are but the fleeting images in our mental conception of the eternal realities which must for ever escape our purely human cognition. But as we see in evolution this progress, in the arms of which we ourselves are enfolded, we may take courage to tread steadily the path which opens before us.

And in this upward path we can afford to

neglect nothing which offers some indication of the lines upon which our further evolution will proceed. In the view of some, amongst them the writer, the material evolution of man has reached nearly to its apex. Its further advance must be psychical. The first few notes of this psychic progress have been sounded. Its continuation lies in the conquest of the field dimly outlined in the Occult Arts, and then on, to heights yet undreamed of, except, perhaps, in the ecstatic visions of prophets and seers, who have found in them possibilities of progress almost, if not quite, incommunicable.

BIBLIOGRAPHY

BELOW is given a list of works which may with advantage be consulted by those who desire fuller information in the various subjects referred to in *The Occult Arts*. The books given are not adduced as authorities from whom the present writer derives his principal support. In some instances it will be found that he differs materially from the conclusions of these other writers. His own work must stand upon the reasonableness of its propositions and the soundness of the arguments used to defend them, or not, as the discriminating reader may decide.

Abnormal Psychology. By Isador H. Coriat. Rider.

Alchemy, Past and Present. By H. Stanley Redgrove. Rider.

Animal Magnetism. By Binet and Feré. International Science Series. Kegan Paul.

Astral Light, The. By Nizida. T.P.S.

Astral Plane, The. By C. W. Leadbeater. Theosophical Publishing Society, 1900.

Building of the Cosmos, The. By Annie Besant. T.P.S., 1911.

Cheiro's Language of the Hand. By Cheiro. Rider.

Cosmic Symbolism. By Sepharial. Rider, 1912.

Drama of Love and Death, The. By Edward Carpenter. George Allen, 1912.

Electricity. What it is? By W. Denham Verschoyle. George Allen, 1908.

Enigmas of Psychical Research. By J. H. Hyslop. Putnam, 1906.

Esoteric Basis of Christianity, The. By William Kingsland. T.P.S., 1895.

Evolution. By E. S. Goodrich. Jack, 1912.

Evolution of Matter, The. By Gustave Le Bon. Walter Scott, 1907.

Five Windows of the Soul, The. By E. H. Aitken. John Murray, 1913.

Foundations of Science, The. By W. C. D. Whetham. Jack, 1912.

Geomancy. By Franz Hartmann. Rider, 1913.

Have you a Strong Will? By Charles Godfrey Leland. Rider.

History of Magic, The. By Eliphas Lévi. Translated, annotated, and introduced by Arthur Edward Waite. Rider, 1913.

Hypnotism. By J. Lawrence. Electric and Magnetic Institute, 1909.

Hypnotism and Suggestion. By Edwin Ash. Rider, 1912.

Hypnotism: Its History, Practice and Theory. By J. M. Bramwell. Rider, 1913.

Isis Unveiled. By H. P. Blavatsky. T.P.S. 2 vols., 1910.

Manual of Occultism, A. By Sepharial. Rider, 1912.

Mathematical Theory of Spirit, A. By H. Stanley Redgrove. Rider.

Miscellanies. By John Aubrey. John Russell Smith, 1857.

Mors Janua Vitæ. By H. A. Dallas. Rider.

Nature's Mysteries. By A. P. Sinnett. T.P.S., 1901.

New Evidences in Psychical Research. By J. Arthur Hill. Rider.

New Knowledge, The. By R. K. Duncan. Hodder & Stoughton, 1905.

New Manual of Astrology, The. By Sepharial. Revised and enlarged edition. Rider.

Occult World, The. By A. P. Sinnett. New York. J. W. Bouton, 1884.

Omens and Superstitions of Southern India. By Edgar Thurston. Unwin, 1912.

Physics of the Secret Doctrine. By William Kingsland. T.P.S., 1910.

BIBLIOGRAPHY

Physiological-Psychology. By W. M'Dougall. J. M. Dent. 2nd edition, 1908.

Plant Animals. By Frederick Keeble. Cambridge University Press, 1910.

Problems of Men, Mind, and Morals (Chapter III.). By Belfort Bax. Grant Richards, 1912.

Psychic Phenomena. By T. J. Hudson. Putnam, 1900.

Psychic Philosophy, as the Foundation of a Religion of Natural Causes. By V. C. Desertis. Rider.

Psycho-Pathological Researches. By Boris Sidis. Rider.

Psychopathy. By Benjamin Rush. William Richmond. Rogers Park, Ill., U.S.A., 1890.

Science and the Infinite. By Sydney D. Klein. Rider, 1912.

Second Sight. By Sepharial. Rider.

Secret Doctrine, The. By H. P. Blavatsky. T.P.S. 3 vols., 1893.

Seven Principles of Man, The. By Annie Besant. T.P.S., 1909.

Spiritual Therapeutics. By W. J. Colville. Chicago. Educ. Pub. Coy., 1888.

Sree Krishna, the Lord of Love. By Bábá Premánand Bhárati. Rider.

Theosophy and the New Psychology. By Annie Besant. T.P.S., 1904.

World Beautiful, The. 2nd series. By Lilian Whiting. Boston : Roberts Bros., 1897.

PRINTED BY NEILL AND CO., LTD., EDINBURGH.

www.ingramcontent.com/pod-product-compliance
Lightning Source LLC
Chambersburg PA
CBHW060316260626
47160CB00007B/2626